wedding
dream
cakes

contents

credits

creative director
Mark Radoha

supervising editor
Veveca Rising

senior art director
Richard Tracy

cake designer
Steve Rocco

senior cake decorator
Susan Matusiak

cake decorators
Mary Gavenda
Nancy Suffolk Guerine
Judy Wysocki
Diane Knowlton
Jayne Mehan

editor
Jeff Shankman

writers
Mary Enochs
Marita Seiler

project manager
Dorri Blank

production coordinator
Mary Stahulak

production studio
Marek/Janci Design

photography
Peter Dean Ross

set designer
Carey Thornton

UNITED STATES
Wilton Industries, Inc.
2240 West 75th Street
Woodridge, IL 60517
Customer Orders: 800-794-5866
Fax: 888-824-9520
E-mail address: orders@wilton.com
For the location of the nearest Wilton cake decorating class, please call 800-942-8881.

CANADA
Wilton Industries, Canada, Ltd.
98 Carrier Drive, Etobicoke, Ontario
M9W 5R1 Canada
Phone: (416) 679-0790
Fax: (416) 679-0798
E-mail address: canadasales@wilton.ca
For the location of the nearest Wilton cake decorating class, please call 416-679-0790.

EUROPE
Wilton Industries/Europe, Inc.
Unit 8 Axis/Hawkfield Business Park
Whitchurch, Bristol BS14OBY England
Phone: 44 (0) 117 9465777
Fax: 44 (0) 117 9465888
For the location of the nearest Wilton cake decorating class, please call 44 (0) 117 9465777.

There is a dream cake for every couple. When you find it, you will know. It's the cake that captures you best—the ultimate expression of your feelings on the most important day of your life.

Wilton *Wedding Dream Cakes* makes finding that perfect cake an exciting part of your wedding day planning. This is our most diverse and beautiful collection ever, reflecting a new freedom in wedding cake design.

There are no limits to wedding cakes today. In *Wedding Dream Cakes*, you will see that virtually anything is possible in the color, shape and style of your cake. If you dream of something bold and contemporary, be sure to see our spectacular "Wildest Dreams" cake, which grabs the eye with fun combinations of pastels and geometric accents—topped by an explosion of stars. If you hold tightly to tradition, *Wedding Dream Cakes* presents many classic floral cakes, made even more appealing with new details such as topiary accents or a canopy of roses.

Wedding Dream Cakes also features many of today's most popular and meaningful themes to use throughout your reception. Butterflies and swans are just two of the beautiful designs on display. Whatever mood you want to set, from romantic to spiritual to lighthearted, there is a cake for you. But don't limit yourself to one big wedding cake. *Wedding Dream Cakes* has exciting ideas for elegant centerpiece cakes, individual guest cakes and chocolate groom's cakes.

Use the complete wedding product section and the special pull-out planning guide inside to help make your perfect day happen. *Wedding Dream Cakes* will inspire you to create the wedding of your dreams.

Vince Naccarato

Vince Naccarato
Chairman and CEO
Wilton Industries, Inc.

dream
cakes
&
you

Apart from you and the groom, the
cake will be the main attraction at
your wedding reception. The
themes and colors you choose,
along with the flowers and accents,
all create one of the day's most
lasting memories.

Selecting the cake is one of your
happiest tasks in planning a wedding. Enjoy browsing through the
following pages. . .discover the
cake of your dreams and enjoy a
perfect wedding day.

love doves

Doves are a favorite wedding image, appearing on everything from invitations to cake tops. They symbolize commitment for life because in the wild they select partners for life. Here, the classic doves accent a traditional tiered cake decorated with contemporary flair.

Cake Serves 243

Features "Spring Song" Ornament and Push-In Pillar and Stacked Construction.

CAKE PREPARATION: Bake and cool 2-layer 6 in., 10 in., 14 in. and 18 in. cakes. For the 18 in. Half Round, you'll need four cakes, stacked together to form two full round layers. Ice smooth and prepare the cakes for Push-In Pillar and Stacked Construction (see page 108). Cover the 10 in., 14 in. and 18 in. cakes with tip 1B stars; it's best to work from bottom to top—that way it will be easier to pipe the stars in an interlocking fashion without creating uneven gaps. Next, cover the sides of the 6 in. cake with tip 1B stars, but leave the top smooth—that's where your ornament will sit.

Make 8 to 10 ribbon bows: Cut white ribbon into strips measuring about 50 in. long. Fold the strips to create four loops and two streamers and secure with florist wire. Next, trim the ends into a chevron shape.

AT THE RECEPTION: Attach Small Doves accents to pillars with dots of icing. Position the ornament[+], the bows and your favorite fresh flowers.

[+]*Warning: Always place a separator plate on the cake before you position any figurine or ornament. This protects both the cake and your keepsake. For extra stability, secure your figurine or ornament to the plate with tacky craft tape.*

(For a complete product listing, see page 123.)

soft as gossamer

There are more ways to decorate a wedding cake than simply adding icing flowers. Our "Soft As Gossamer" design uses the popular European light yellow rolled fondant to give the cake a soft, smooth elegance accented with tulle and floral pearl sprays.

Cake Serves 72*
Features "First Dance" Figurine and Push-in Pillar Construction.

ADVANCE WORK: The 79 tulle puffs that decorate this cake can be made well before decorating the cake. There are 4 styles of puffs to make: 33 accented with Hanging Lily Spray (pull cluster of 3 apart to use 1 spray for each puff), 22 accented with Lily Pearl Sprays, 20 accented with White Pearl Sprays and 4 plain puffs to decorate the top of the cake. To make puffs, spread a tulle circle flat on work surface, fold in half and place your accent piece at the center. Gather the circle at the center to form a puff, secure at gathering point with florist wire and wrap with florist tape. Set aside.

Make your flowers several days in advance. Use royal icing, flower nail no. 9 and tip 101 to make 50 apple blossoms with tip 2 dot centers. Make extras to allow for breakage and let dry.

CAKE PREPARATION: Tint 5 pks. of fondant yellow to cover cakes and reserve 1 pk. of white fondant for drape. Bake and cool 1-layer 7 in., 11 in. and 15 in. cakes, torted and filled to create 3 in. high tiers. Prepare for rolled fondant by icing lightly with buttercream. Prepare for push-in pillar construction (see page 107). Cover with fondant and smooth with Easy Glide Smoothers. Use craft knife to cut hidden pillars

to 5 in. long. Assemble cakes. Pipe tip 5 bead bottom borders in buttercream on all cakes.

For drape, roll out and cut the following fondant pieces: 12 x 5 in. for 7 in. cake, 14 x 5 in. for 11 in. cake, 16 x 7 in. for 15 in. cake. Gather pieces to form drapes, pinch ends together to hold shape. Use a decorator brush to spread water on back of each drape, then attach to cakes. Cut 5 in. wide lengths of tulle and attach to drapes with softened pieces of fondant. Attach apple blossoms to drape using royal icing and tip 2. Cut cake circles to fit centers of 11 in. and 15 in. cakes; cover circles with reserved yellow fondant. Attach tulle puffs to center circle area and underneath cake plates with royal icing, making sure wire does not penetrate cakes.

AT THE RECEPTION: Make sure puffs are secure; position figurine.[+]

*Note: The top tier is often saved for the first anniversary. The number of servings given does not include the top tier.

[+]Warning: Always place a separator plate on the cake before you position any figurine or ornament. This protects both the cake and your keepsake. For extra stability, secure your figurine or ornament to the plate with tacky craft tape.

(For a complete product listing, see page 123.)

Features "Blush Rose Topiary" Ornament with Center Column Construction.

ADVANCE WORK: At least one week prior to decorating, make 45 lattice pieces using royal icing: Cut paper to fit large flower former. Draw 1 1/2 x 3 1/2 in. rectangle patterns on formers. Tape waxed paper over flower former, then spray with a thin coating of vegetable oil pan spray for easy removal later. After spraying, wipe lightly with tissue to remove excess. Pipe tip 3 outline and lattice; add tip 3 bead borders. Make extras to allow for breakage and let dry.

A few days in advance, using royal icing, make 1000 tip 103 sweet peas; 375 tip 102 sweet peas and 92 tip 101 roses with tip 5 bases on Flower Nail No. 9. (Combine Pink and Creamy Peach icing colors to achieve shade used for roses.) Make extras, let dry.

CAKE PREPARATION: To support ornament, cut a 4 in. cardboard circle and wrap in foil; set aside. Bake and cool 2-layer 6 in., 10 in. (5 needed) and 14 in. cakes. Prepare for Lady Windermere Center Column Construction with the Tall Tier Stand (see page 109).

On four bottom 10-in. cakes: Divide each into 8ths on top. Pipe tip 18 elongated shell on side at each division point; position clusters of tip 102 sweet peas in cascade over shell. Using ruler, mark lattice area 1 1/2 in. from bottom of cake; pipe tip 2 lattice. Edge top of lattice with tip 3 beads. Pipe tip 18 zigzag top and bottom borders; position tip 103 sweet peas and roses; pipe tip 352 leaves.

Next, decorate 14 in. cake: Divide into 8ths. Pipe tip 18 elongated shell, 1 1/2 in. long, on side of cake at division points. Pipe tip 18 zigzag top border. Position tip 102 sweet peas in cascade over shells; position tip 103 sweet peas and roses at top border. Attach angels

centered between flower cascades on cake sides. Pipe tip 18 shell bottom border. Pipe tip 18 zigzags between lattice pieces (lattice pieces will be attached at reception); position tip 103 sweet peas. Pipe tip 352 leaves.

On 10 in. center cake: Divide into 8ths; mark garland area 1 1/2 in. deep. Pipe tip 18 zigzag garland from division points. Pipe tip 5 bead top border. Add tip 18 zigzag bottom border. Position tip 102 and 103 sweet peas on garlands and bottom border; position roses at garland points; add tip 352 leaves.

On 6 in. cake: Divide into 4ths. Pipe tip 18 elongated shells on side of cake at division points. Pipe tip 18 zigzag top border. Position tip 102 sweet peas in cascade over shells; position tip 103 sweet peas and roses at top border. Pipe tip 352 leaves. Position petite cherubs, between cascades, on cake sides. Position dowel rods into cake to support ornament. Bottom border and lattice will be completed at reception.

AT THE RECEPTION: Assemble 4-arm base following directions on page 101, then add bottom column bolt and 13 1/2 in. column. Position 16 in. plate onto 13 1/2 in. base column section and tightly screw on 7 3/4 in. column. Carefully position lattice pieces on sides and on tops of cakes. Continue adding tiers with columns. At top plate, secure columns with cap nut bolt. Position top tier cake and decorate bottom border with tip 18 zigzags and add lattice pieces and sweet peas with tip 352 leaves. Position covered cake board on top of 6 in. cake and place ornament on top. Position fresh flowers.

*Note: The top tier is often saved for the first anniversary. The number of servings given does not include the top tier.

(For a complete product listing, see page 123.)

The topiary look is the latest trend in cake ornaments. On "A Dance of Angels," the Blush Rose Topiary crowns a cake decorated with ever-popular angels. Together, the flowers and angels create a romantic Victorian effect.

a dance of angels

ADVANCE WORK: Make the bow loops which will top each cake: For the 6 in. cake, you will need 12 strips each of silver and gold wired ribbon, 5 1/2 in. long. Fold silver strips into loops and attach with tip 2 and royal icing; Repeat with gold strips, attaching over the top of the silver strips to make 12 loops. For the 10 in. cake, you'll need 16 strips each of silver and gold wired ribbon, 7 in. long, to make 16 loops; for the 14 in. cake, you'll need 20 strips each, 11 1/4 in. long, to make 20 loops. Assemble loops as above and set aside.

CAKE PREPARATION: Bake and cool 2-layer 6, 10 and 14 in. round cakes. Prepare cakes for rolled fondant by covering with buttercream. Cover with fondant and smooth with Easy-Glide Smoothers.

For 6 in. tier, use the Cake Dividing Set to divide cake into 8ths, then divide each section into 4ths, for a total of 32 sections. Cut 16 6 in. lengths of 4 mm pearls, and 8 6 in. lengths each of silver and gold ribbon. Attach with royal icing to cake side in alternating pearl/silver ribbon/pearl/gold ribbon pattern. Twist double strands, 22 in. long, of 6 mm pearl beads together with gold ribbon and attach to bottom border with royal icing.

For 10 in. tier, use Cake Dividing Set to divide cake into 16ths and then into halves for a total of 32 sections. Cut 16 8 1/2 in. lengths of 4 mm pearls, and 8 lengths each of silver and gold ribbon. Attach with royal icing as on 6 in. tier. Twist double strands, 35 in. long, of 6 mm pearl beads together with gold ribbon and attach to bottom border with royal icing.

For 14 in. tier, use Cake Dividing Set to divide cake into 12ths and then into 4ths for a total of 48 sections. Cut 24 11 in. lengths of 4 mm pearls, and 12 11 in. lengths each of silver and gold ribbon. Attach to cake side with royal icing as above. Twist double strands, 50 in. long, of 6 mm pearl beads together with gold ribbon and attach to bottom border with royal icing.

For all cakes, assemble loops into bow, attaching at center with tip 4 and royal icing.

AT THE RECEPTION: Position cakes on stand and position figurine on top. Decorate table using 15 additional packages of 4 mm and 6 mm pearls.

*Note: The top tier is often saved for the first anniversary. The number of servings given does not include the top tier.

(For a complete product listing, see page 123.)

silver and gold

Traditional colors of wealth, silver and gold will be even more prominent in the new millennium. As theme colors, they add brilliance and sophistication to your wedding day. At the wedding service, decorate the seating with silver and gold ribbon. At the reception, decorate tables with silver and gold favors and place cards.

ADVANCE WORK: Prepare the color flow scallop pieces, the royal icing wild roses and bachelor buttons—they will need several days to dry before positioning. You will need four each of the small, medium and large scallop pieces; the patterns shown on pages 118-119 are for quarters. To make color flow pieces: Tape patterns to cake boards, cover with waxed paper. Use tip 2 and a parchment bag half filled with full-strength color flow icing to outline patterns; when outline is set, flow in with tip 2 and thinned down color flow. On another sheet of waxed paper, pipe a total of 120 tip 2 dots in three different sizes and let dry. When color flow pieces are dry, randomly attach dried color flow dots with icing. While color flow pieces are still on cake board, pipe tip 2 beads on inner and outer borders. Use tip 2 to pipe dot flowers and vines. Let dry completely.

Using royal icing, make 20 tip 104 white wild roses with tip 2 white pull-out stamens. Make 110 white bachelor buttons using tips 1, 4 and 13. Make extras of all flowers to allow for breakage and let dry.

CAKE PREPARATION: Bake and cool 2-layer 9 in., 12 in. and 15 in.

cakes. Ice smooth with spatula and prepare for push-in pillar construction (see page 107); position on plates. Add tip 4 bead borders to top, bottom and corners of all cakes. Pipe tip 4 dot flowers on cake sides. Position color flow base pieces at bottom of 15 in. cake. Add tip 4 bead bottom border and position 3 wild roses and artificial leaves at each corner.

AT THE RECEPTION: Insert pillars into cake and pipe tip 4 dots around base of pillars. Carefully position color flow pieces onto mini marshmallows (cut in half) on tops of all cakes. Attach bachelor buttons to color flow pieces. Position Circle of Love Topper and four floral puff accents on middle tier, six on bottom tier. Position ornament.[+]

*Note: The top tier is often saved for the first anniversary. The number of servings given does not include the top tier.

[+]Warning: Always place a separator plate on the cake before you position any figurine or ornament. This protects both the cake and your keepsake. For extra stability, secure your figurine or ornament to the plate with tacky craft tape.

(For a complete product listing, see page 123.)

Holding on to tradition while adding touches of the contemporary is perfectly natural for today's brides. This cake's hexagon shape with extending scallops creates a distinctive look to complement any wedding theme.

silhouette inscallops

luscious
fruits

For outdoor or afternoon weddings, a light wedding cake featuring whipped cream and fresh strawberries is sure to please you and your guests. This cake will work with most fruits—you can substitute raspberries, blackberries or a mixture of fruit. Ask your caterer for an arrangement of fresh fruits to complement the cake.

Cake Serves 156*
Features the Garden Cake Stand.

CAKE PREPARATION: Bake and cool 2-layer 8 in., 12 in. and 16 in. cakes. Ice smooth with whipped topping. Use tip 104 to pipe a continuous ribbon effect, resembling cornelli lace, over all cakes. On cake tops, position a Crystal-Look Bowl upside down at center. Ice bowl and position fresh strawberries, raspberries, blueberries and mint leaves. Add fruit and leaves to bottom borders.

AT THE RECEPTION: Decorate Garden Cake Stand with fresh greens. Wrap lollipop sticks with green floral tape; insert sticks into strawberries and tape to stand.

*Note: The top tier is often saved for the first anniversary. The number of servings given does not include the top tier.

(For a complete product listing, see page 123.)

ADVANCE WORK: One week in advance, make the following using melted Light Cocoa Premium Candy Melts®+: Mold a candy box lid and bottom, filling to top of the molds. Pipe tip 2 zigzag garland and dot trim on inside of lid when firm. Mold 140 truffles, pipe a swirl on top of each and mold 64 hearts. Using the heart pans, mold 6, 9 and 12 in. candy plaques, filling 1/4 in. deep. Set aside.

Plates will not be used on the stand, so you will need to make heart-shaped cake boards. Use double thick cake boards, cut into heart shapes and covered with Fanci-Foil Wrap. Use the pans as an outline, but be certain to allow about 2 in. extra space for the bottom borders.

CAKE PREPARATION: Bake and cool 2-layer 91/4, 121/2 and 141/4 in. cakes. Ice smooth in chocolate buttercream icing. Comb sides. Position candy plaques on cake tops—6 in. on 91/4 in. tier, 9 in. on 121/2 in. tier, 12 in. on 141/4 in. tier. Decorate all cakes as follows: Pipe tip 21 shell top border and tip 127D ruffle on top edge. Add tip 21 shell border between ruffle and plaque. Pipe tip 21 rosette bottom border. Position truffles on 121/2 and 141/4 in. cakes. Begin at the heart point and work back. Place candy hearts around bottom border on alternating rosettes on all tiers. Begin at the heart point and work back around each side of the cake.

Assemble the cake top ornament. Position the candy plaque lid on the box bottom at an angle. Secure with melted candy and hold in place until set. Position figurine and truffles.

AT THE RECEPTION: Position tiers on stand, so that they sit slightly askew on the stand for a stairstep effect. Position figurine on top tier.

Centerpieces

ADVANCE WORK: Make the following using melted Premium Candy Melts: Mold 2 heart box tops; 2 double swans; 2 double bells using fondant mold; 12 deep heart truffles using your favorite candy filling; 13 truffles. Pipe tip 2 swirl on top of truffles. Make candy plaques using 6 in. Round Pan, filled to 1/2 depth and Singles! Fancy Ring Mold, filled to 1/3 depth.

Assemble centerpiece using dots of melted candy:

Sandwich heart box tops back-to-back, attach double swans and double bells to each side. Pipe tip 2 bead border around edge. Attach Fancy Ring Mold plaque on top of 6 in. Round Pan plaque; position heart upright in center, securing with dots of candy. Using tip 2, pipe zigzag garland around edge of round plaque; add bead bottom border.

AT THE RECEPTION: Position truffles on plaque and arrange heart truffles around base.

+*brand confectionery coating*

*Note: The top tier is often saved for the first anniversary. The number of servings given does not include the top tier.

(For a complete product listing, see page 123.)

chocolate
bliss

These truffle-topped tiers are a chocolate lover's dream. Continue the truffle theme at your reception with a decadent swan chocolate box filled with truffles at each guest table. And send guests home with a sweet remembrance of the day—a petite favor box containing a pair of truffles.

serene swans

The swan's graceful shape, along with its practice of choosing a lifetime partner, make it an ideal wedding motif. You can easily coordinate the look at the table, as swans are often used as part of candles and favors. Include the cake's wonderful shade of blue in your table decorating, too.

Cake Serves 124*
Features "Exuberance" Ornament, Pearl Swans and Push-In Pillar Construction.

ADVANCE WORK: Make the following several days in advance using royal icing: 166 tip 2F blue drop flowers with tip 3 white dot centers; 34 tip 68 white ruffled swags 3 in. wide x 1³/4 in. deep; 112 tip 129 white drop flowers with tip 3 white dot centers. Make extras of all to allow for breakage and let dry.

Note: Combine violet and royal blue icing colors to produce the periwinkle blue for the flowers.

CAKE PREPARATION: Bake and cool 2-layer 9¹/4 in. and 12¹/2 in. heart tiers, 3 in. high; 2-layer 14¹/4 in. heart tier 4 in. high. Using buttercream icing, ice tops smooth in blue and sides in white. Prepare for push-in pillar construction (see page 107).

Decorate all tiers the same. Pipe tip 17 shell bottom border. Position blue drop flowers on shells. Next, add tip 17 reverse shell top border. Starting at the heart point, attach ruffle swags to the cake sides, resting bottom of swag on the drop flowers. Attach 3 white drop flowers to each swag point. Position 9 in. push-in pillars in the 14¹/4 in. tier and 7 in. push-in pillars in the 12¹/2 in. tier. Using dots of icing, attach blue drop flowers to the base of each pillar. Next, attach blue and white drop flowers randomly to tops of 14¹/4 in. and 12¹/2 in. tiers.

AT THE RECEPTION: Assemble tiers on pillars. Position swans on 14¹/4 and 12¹/2 in. tiers, place Exuberance ornament on top of 9¹/4 in. tier.⁺

*Note: The top tier is often saved for the first anniversary. The number of servings given does not include the top tier.

⁺Warning: Always place a separator plate on the cake before you position any figurine or ornament. This protects both the cake and your keepsake. For extra stability, secure your figurine or ornament to the plate with tacky craft tape.

(For a complete product listing, see page 123.)

joined
in splendor

When wedding bells ring, you declare your love to the world. This cake, featuring bells and the full bridal party, is in perfect harmony with your theme colors. Both the flowers and the bridesmaids support the colors you have selected for your special day.

Cake Serves 262*
Features "Dedication" Ornament and Plate and Pillar Construction.

ADVANCE WORK: The charming scrolls which crown each tier of this design should be made several days in advance. We simply overpiped our plastic scrolls with tip 13 and royal icing—piping one side, letting dry completely, then repeating on the other side. When completely dry, pipe two tip 13 pull-out spikes, 2^1/$_2$ in. long, on back side. Make extra scrolls to allow for breakage.

CAKE PREPARATION: Bake and cool three 8 in., two 12 in. and one 16 in. 2-layer cakes, ice smooth. Prepare for plate and pillar construction (see page 107). Using Cake Dividing Set, divide 8 in. cakes into 4ths, 12 in. cakes into 6ths and 16 in. cake into 8ths. Decorate all the cakes as follows: Position two scrolls at division points. Mark cake for drop strings, with the largest measuring 1^1/$_2$ in. from bottom of cake, side strings measuring 2^3/$_4$ in. from bottom of cake. Pipe tip 13 drop strings below scrolls. Add tip 13 rosettes and fleurs de lis at beginning points of drop strings. Pipe tip 21 rosette bottom borders; overpipe rosettes with tip 13 diagonal zigzags.

To decorate the stairways, cut four 9 in. x 27 in. lengths of tulle and attach to stairs with florist wire, twisting and turning through the stair openings. Attach silk flowers to tulle and 1 in. bells to sides of stairs with hot glue. Remove top portion of Romantic Heart Base; attach flower girl and ring bearer to top with hot glue. Attach two 2^1/$_4$ in. bells to florist wire, then attach to underside of plates with hot glue.

AT THE RECEPTION: Assemble cakes and add final decorating touches. Add fresh flowers to flower holder ring; position fountain. Position cakes and stairs to form semicircle around fountain and add bridesmaids, groomsmen and ornament.[+]

*Note: The top tier is often saved for the first anniversary. The number of servings given does not include the top tier.

[+]Warning: Always place a separator plate on the cake before you position any figurine or ornament. This protects both the cake and your keepsake. For extra stability, secure your topper to the plate with tacky craft tape.

(For a complete product listing, see page 124.)

The rose remains a favorite flower for weddings and the most popular flower symbolizing love. Your rose theme can encompass a variety of colors from pure white to soft yellow, as used on this cake. No matter the color, a cake abundant in roses will add beauty and distinction to your wedding.

rich in roses

Features "Candlelight Ivory Romance" Ornament and Push-in Pillar and Stacked Construction.

ADVANCE WORK: Make flowers at least 2 to 3 days in advance. This cake features more than 20 dozen royal icing roses—because royal icing flowers keep indefinitely when stored properly, it's a good idea to allow more time to make them. Be sure to make extras in case of breakage and store them in a cool dark area to avoid fading. These are full-bloom roses, with a top row of three petals, a middle row of five petals and a bottom row of seven petals.

On flower nail no. 7, make tip 103 roses with tip 10 bases and tip 104 roses with tip 12 bases: For each size,

make 31 light yellow, 31 medium yellow, 31 dark yellow and 31 white. Let dry.

CAKE PREPARATION: Bake and cool 7³/4 x 5⁵/8 in., 10³/4 x 7 ⁵/8 in., 13 x 9 ⁷/8 in. oval cakes, torted and layered to create 3 in. high cakes and 2-layer (4 in. high) 16 ¹/2 x 12 ³/8 in. oval cake. Use spatula to ice cakes with swirl motion and prepare for push-in pillar and stacked construction (see page 107). Pipe tip 6 bead bottom border on top two tiers. Randomly position roses on top three tiers and completely cover bottom cake with roses. Add tip 352 leaves to roses.

AT THE RECEPTION: Assemble cakes and position ornament.⁺

*Note: The top tier is often saved for the first anniversary. The number of servings given does not include the top tier.

⁺Warning: Always place a separator plate on the cake before you position any figurine or ornament. This protects both the cake and your keepsake. For extra stability, secure your topper to the plate with tacky craft tape.

(For a complete product listing, see page 124.)

happy trails

If the American West is your vision of the perfect wedding locale, our stagecoach can take you there. Built from gum paste pieces, it crosses two fondant tiers, which feature a rugged horizon above and a roped and fringed garland below.

Cake Serves 175*

Features "Country & Western" Figurine and Plate and Pillar Construction.

ADVANCE WORK: Building the stagecoach[+] will be easy if you follow the patterns and allow at least a week or two in advance for proper drying. The pattern pieces (pages 121-122) are clearly marked and keyed to fit together as you would a model airplane—you'll be attaching the gum paste pieces with hot glue.

First, glue pattern pieces to poster board and cut out (the additional thickness of poster board will reinforce the pattern). Set aside. Mix an entire can of gum paste, tinting half light ivory and leaving the remaining half white. Roll out ivory gum paste $1/8$ in. thick and cut out stagecoach parts, horse and wheels. Dry on flat surface that is lightly dusted with cornstarch. Dry pieces on one side for a day, then turn and dry for one more day. The pieces should be completely dry and hard. On the two coach side pieces, mark a guideline with a light pencil, following the dotted line on the pattern. This is the point where pieces should be attached. See page 121 for stagecoach assembly instructions. For Horse: Attach legs to opposite side of horse, offset slightly to create a 3D effect. Pipe tip 2 pull-out mane and tail. Dust with grated non-toxic artist chalk using a decorator brush. Cut a $21/2$ x $11/2$ in. gum paste oval base for figurine. Set aside to dry.

CAKE PREPARATION: Bake and cool one each, 2-layer 13 x 9$7/8$ in. oval, 14 in. square and 14 in. round cakes. To create bottom cake, cut 14 in. round in half and place on either side of 14 in. square cake to form large oval. Prepare for plate and pillar construction (see page 107). Tint 1 package of fondant medium brown, $1/3$ package green, leave $2/3$ package white and combine with remainder of white gum paste. Tint the remaining 8 packages ivory.

Prepare cakes with buttercream and cover with ivory fondant; smooth with Easy-Glide Smoothers. Divide bottom tier into 8 sections by wrapping a 3 in. high band of waxed paper around bottom of cake and folding it four times. While waxed paper is still folded, cut in a scallop design. The top peak of scallop should measure $21/2$ in. high, the lowest $11/2$ in. high. When fully opened, the waxed paper will have 16 peaks. Place waxed paper on cake sides and trace scallops with toothpick; this will serve as a guide for positioning rope and fringe. Pipe tip 4 bead bottom border. Make fringe pieces (cut, attach and trim one at a time): Roll out the white fondant mixed with gum paste $1/8$ in. thick. Cut into 1 in. wide x 3 in. deep rectangular section. Using scissors,

fringe the section by cutting $1/8$ in. wide strips vertically almost to the top edge. Do not cut all the way through. Attach fringe to cake side along your marked area using dots of royal icing. Trim any excess fringe even with your cake board. Next, make 16 ropes for garland: Roll brown fondant into 12-in. long strand; fold in half and twist. Attach to top of fringe with royal icing. Twist small pieces of rope to resemble a knot and attach at garland points with royal icing.

For cactus scene on top tier, roll brown fondant $1/8$ in. thick. Cut mountain strips, in various heights from 1 to 1$3/4$ in.. Attach to border of cake with brush strokes of water, smooth edges together. Roll green fondant $1/4$ in. thick. Using pattern (p. 122), cut cactus shapes. Attach around border with water, smooth with finger. Using edge of tapered spatula, mark lines in cactus. Using buttercream icing, pipe tip 1 pull-out dot needles.

Mark where horse's legs will be positioned on cake top and make holes in cake with lollipop stick. Cut lollipop sticks in half and attach to right front and back legs of horse with royal icing. Insert sticks in cake. Position coach and couple on base next to horse.

AT THE RECEPTION: Assemble cake; add fresh flowers to bowl and position on oval separator plate between cake tiers.

[+]*For a time-saving decorating option, replace the stagecoach and horse with additional fondant cactus shapes. Attach cactus pieces to lollipop sticks with icing, let dry and insert sticks in cake.*

**Note: The top tier is often saved for the first anniversary. The number of servings given does not include the top tier.*

(For a complete product listing, see page 124.)

Since the beginning of time, candles have set a mood that is intimate, romantic and dramatic. Candles are a simple, inexpensive way to create atmosphere. Carry your candlelight theme throughout the reception by using candles as the centerpiece at each guest table and at the place card table.

aglow in candlelight

Cake Serves 272*

Features "Lace Charm" Ornament and Stacked Construction.

CAKE PREPARATION: Bake and cool 2-layer 8 in., 10 in., 12 in., 14 in. and 16 in. cakes. Ice smooth and prepare for stacked construction (see page 106). Mark the cakes to pipe your strings and garlands, using the Cake Dividing Set: Divide the 8 in., 10 in. and 12 in. cakes into 8ths; divide the 14 in. and 16 in. cakes into 16ths.

On 8 in. and 10 in. cakes, pipe tip 3 triple drop strings at division points, measuring 1 in., 2 in. and $2^1/2$ in. deep from top edge of cake; stagger the bottom drop string on the 8 in. cake at $2^1/4$ and $2^1/2$ in. deep. On 12 in., 14 in. and 16 in. cakes, pipe a tip 17 zigzag garland from division points, measuring 2 in. deep. On

12 in. cake, pipe tip 3 triple drop strings measuring 1 in., 2 in. and 3 in. deep from top edge of cake; stagger the bottom drop string at $2^1/4$ and 3 in. deep. On the 14 in. cake, pipe tip 3 triple drop strings measuring 1 in., 2 in. and 3 in. deep. On the 16 in. cake pipe tip 3 quadruple drop strings measuring $1/2$ in., 1 in., 2 in. and 3 in. deep.

On all cakes, using tip 17, pipe a shell top border and a zigzag puff bottom border. Add tip 3 dots where strings meet on 8 in., 10 in. and 12 in. cakes. Add tip 17 rosettes where strings meet on 14 in. and 16 in. cakes.

AT THE RECEPTION: Position ornament, candles and fresh flowers.

Be sure to use non-drip pillar candles from 3 in. to 6 in. high and surround them with fresh flowers only. Do not use dried or silk flowers. For safety, use foil bases or glass candle holders.

*Note: The top tier is often saved for the first anniversary. The number of servings given does not include the top tier.

(For a complete product listing, see page 124.)

ADVANCE WORK: Make gum paste roses and leaves at least 4 days in advance. Use one can of gum paste mix along with cutters and directions in Rose Bouquet Set to make 8 full bloom roses, 16 medium roses, 16 rosebuds and 140 leaves. (Make all flowers on toothpicks.) Make extras to allow for breakage and let dry.

To prepare cake board or plywood base pattern, position one 10 in. round cake board in center and place eight 6 in. round cake boards around center 10 in. board. Be sure to leave 1/4 in. between each 6 in. cake. Trace boards, then cut 1 1/2 in. larger around all sides; cover with foil and set aside. We've also raised the entire cake 3 in. off the table for a floating effect. To do this, position a piece of wood as large as the base of the cake, covered in foil.

CAKE PREPARATION: Bake and cool eight 2-layer 6 in. round cakes, one 2-layer 10 in. round cake and one 2-layer 15 in. petal cake. Prepare for stacked construction (see page 106). Prepare cakes for rolled fondant by lightly icing with buttercream. Cover cakes with rolled fondant and smooth with Easy-Glide Smoothers. Insert dowel rods into 10 in. cake and position in center of board. Position 6 in. round cakes on board. Use petal pan as a guide to mark where cake will rest on 6 in. cakes; dowel rod 6 in. cakes in those areas. Position 15 in. petal cake and dowel rod in center for 10 in. plate.

Mold fondant garlands and roses using Romance Accents Fondant Mold and position immediately on all cakes using a damp brush. (It's important to make each garland and rose as you are ready to apply it to cake.

Each piece needs to be pliable to conform to the shape of the cake). On petal cake, place a fondant rose on cake top at each petal point; position 3 additional roses in garland formation, 2 1/2 in. deep on cake sides. On 6 in. cakes, position fondant garlands 2 1/4 in. deep.

Roll 3/8 in. diameter fondant ropes and position around bottom borders of 6 in. and petal cakes. On petal cake, position additional fondant garlands at a "beveled" angle over rope border; edge with tip 2 dots. On 6 in. cakes, pipe 13 evenly-spaced tip 2 strings (pipe center string first, then add 6 more to both sides of center) on tops and sides to meet garlands. Add tip 2 dot at each end. Pipe tip 2 drop string garlands

from bottom of fondant garlands; position fondant rose on each cake top. Insert gum paste roses on toothpicks in rope borders around 6 in. cakes; add leaves.

AT THE RECEPTION: position 10 in. plate and separator ring; assemble fountain. Using tacky wax, attach Lovebirds ornament and small doves to fountain.[+]

*Note: The smallest tier is often saved for the first anniversary. The number of servings given does not include one 6 in. top tier.

[+]Warning: Always place a separator plate on the cake before you position any figurine or ornament. This protects both the cake and your keepsake. For extra stability, secure your topper to the plate with tacky craft tape.

(For a complete product listing, see page 124.)

Fountains have traditionally been placed at the bottom of the cake beneath the cake layers. This design places the fountain on top, so that its flowing water and illumination can highlight the cake. Fountains can also be placed off to the side and decorated with doves or flowers to tie in with your wedding theme.

fountain
fantasy

cakes
for everyone

Individual guest cakes can be modeled after the larger wedding cake or can be designed based on the wedding theme. Hearts, roses, chocolate—any theme can be used. Display them all on a cake table prior to serving and have them served after dinner or use as table centerpieces.

"Dawn of Romance" Serves 116
Features "Bianca" Figurine and Stacked Construction.

ADVANCE WORK: Use Gum Paste Mix and rose leaf cutter from Rose Bouquet Set to make 200 white leaves. Make extras to allow for breakage and let dry.

CAKE PREPARATION: Bake and cool 2-layer 7 in., 10 in. and 14 in. cakes, each 1¹/2 in. deep to form 3 in. high tiers. Ice smooth and prepare for stacked construction (see page 106). Use tip 2 to randomly pipe vines on tops and sides. Attach leaves to vines. Pipe tip 7 bead bottom borders.

AT THE RECEPTION: Position ornament on separator plate. Position fresh flowers.

*Note: The top tier is often saved for the first anniversary. The number of servings given does not include the top tier.

"Flowing Vines"
Use gum paste mix (tinted royal blue/violet combination) and floral ejector set to make 13 flowers for each mini cake. Make extras to allow

for breakage and let dry. When dry, pipe tip 2 dot centers in buttercream (use remaining icing from main cake). Let dry.

CAKE PREPARATION: Bake and cool 1 each standard and mini cupcakes (without baking cups) for each mini cake. Line jelly roll pan with parchment paper; position cooling grid on top of parchment paper. Place cupcake and mini cupcake upside down on rack. Heat ready-to-use icing in can to pourable consistency. Pour icing over cupcakes; gently tap grid to evenly distribute icing. Carefully remove cakes with spatula and place on parchment-lined jelly roll pan to dry. When icing is firm to touch, stack mini cupcake on top of standard cupcake. Pipe tip 2 vines on cake tops and sides. Pipe tip 2 bead bottom border around base of cupcake. Position drop flowers on cakes; add tip 349 leaves. Pipe tip 352 leaf bottom border.

(For a complete product listing, see page 124.)

A

B

C

D

E

F

34

A "Loving Couple"

ADVANCE WORK: Use royal icing and tip 129 to make 20 (for each cake) drop flowers with tip 2 dot centers. Make extras to allow for breakage and let dry.

CAKE PREPARATION: Use 4 to 6 cups of cake batter to make 1 in. high cake in 11 x 15 in. sheet pan; bake and cool. Use 3³/4 in. and 3 in. heart cookie cutters to cut 2 "tiers" for each cake. Place cakes on cooling grid positioned over sheet pan. Pour melted Candy Melts® over cakes and position on waxed paper to set. Stack cakes and fill with your favorite fillings; pipe tip 3 bead bottom borders on both cakes. Position flowers; add tip 349 leaves. Position couple.

B "A Single Rose"

ADVANCE WORK: Several days ahead, make Candy Clay rose (see instructions in current *Wilton Yearbook of Cake Decorating*). Set aside. Thoroughly wash and dry rose or lemon leaves. Lighten dark green Candy Melts with a little white. "Paint" top of leaf using decorator brush. Set aside until firm.

CAKE PREPARATION: Bake regular and mini cupcakes with no baking cups. Place upside down on cooling grid positioned over sheet pan. Thin melted candy with solid vegetable shortening and pour over cakes. Gently tap grid to evenly distribute candy. Set cakes on waxed paper to dry. Stack cakes when completely dry. Pipe bead bottom borders with melted candy in cut parchment bag. Pipe dots on sides with melted candy.

Carefully remove real leaf from painted candy leaf. Attach rose and candy leaf with melted candy.

C "Belle Fleurs"

ADVANCE WORK: Several days ahead, use tip 101 and royal icing to make 6 (for each cake) apple blossoms with tip 1 dot centers. Make extras to allow for breakage and let dry. Make ribbon bows and set aside.

CAKE PREPARATION: Use 4 to 6 cups of batter to make 1 in. high cake in 11 x 15 in. sheet pan; bake and cool. Use cookie cutter to cut out bell cakes. Place cakes on cooling grid positioned over sheet pan. Heat canned icing to a pourable consistency and pour over cakes. Tap grid gently to evenly distribute icing. Set cakes aside to cool on waxed paper. When completely dry, pipe tip 2 zigzag garlands and tip 1 dots on cakes. Attach flowers and bows with dots of icing; pipe tip 352 leaves.

D "Signature Heart"

CAKE PREPARATION: Bake and cool mini heart cakes. Place cakes on cooling grid over a jelly roll pan. Make bells using fondant mold dusted with cornstarch; press fondant into mold and release. Heat ready-to-use icing in can to pourable consistency. Tint icing with peach/pink mixture. Place cakes on cooling grid positioned over sheet pan. Pour icing over cakes; gently tap cooling grid to evenly distribute icing. Let dry on waxed paper. Using buttercream, pipe tip 16 c-motion bottom border. Attach fondant bells. Write tip 2 message.

E "Mini Tiers"

ADVANCE WORK: Cut lollipop sticks in half to measure 3 inches each. Using Candy Melts and Bride & Groom Mold, mold couple and position half lollipop sticks in each. Refrigerate until firm. Use royal icing to make 12 tip 225 drop flowers with tip 3 dot centers. Make extras to allow for breakage and let dry.

CAKE PREPARATION: Use 4 to 6 cups of cake batter to make 1 in. high cake in 11 x 15 in. sheet pan; bake and cool. Cut out mini wedding cakes with Comfort Grip™ cookie cutter. Place cakes on cooling grid positioned over sheet pan. Heat icing to a pourable consistency; add icing color and pour over cakes. Tap grid gently to evenly distribute icing. Set cakes aside to cool on waxed paper. When completely dry, pipe tip 3 double drop string garlands and tip 3 bead borders. Position flowers and candy couple.

F "Doves Devotion"

ADVANCE WORK: Using royal icing, make 10 tip 101s two-tone roses with tip 4 bases on flower nail #9. Make extras to allow for breakage and let dry.

CAKE PREPARATION: Attach petite heart cake on top of mini heart cake with icing. Place cake on grid and cover with poured fondant. Let set. Pipe tip 4 ball bottom borders. Attach roses with dots of icing. Cut stems off of doves and position on cake.

(For a complete product listing, see page 124-125.)

A hot new trend in wedding cakes is serving a simply decorated mini cake to each guest. This can be done in place of a large cake or in addition to a smaller cake for the bride and groom. Either way, everyone loves this personal touch at the table.

cakes for everyone

ADVANCE WORK: Make flowers, scroll designs and color flow Claddagh at least 2 days in advance.

Using royal icing, make approximately 1700 tip 224 drop flowers with tip 2 dot centers; let dry.

Using royal icing, make approximately 14 medium and 16 large scrolls: Trace medium and large scroll pattern presses with pencil on plain paper. Cover drawn patterns with waxed paper and pipe scrolls with tip 17. Make extras to allow for breakage and let dry. When completely dry, attach drop flowers to scrolls with royal icing. Let dry and set aside.

Make color flow Claddagh: Cover pattern (see page122) with waxed paper; using full-strength color flow icing and tip 3, outline pattern, let

dry. Fill in remainder of pattern with thinned color flow icing. When completely dry, turn over, position lollipop stick in center and repeat process on other side. Let dry. On front side, pipe tip 2 lattice on heart, then pipe tip 13 zigzag scallop garland around heart. Pipe tip 3 bead border on heart and tip 2 bead border on crown. Let dry.

CAKE PREPARATION: Bake and cool 8 in. and 12 in. round cakes, torting and filling to create 3 in. tiers. Ice smooth with buttercream. On both 3 in. high cakes, mark 1/4 in. down from top edge and 1/4 in. up from bottom edge on cake sides. Pipe tip 2 lattice on sides using 1/4 in. marks as guides. Add drop flowers to top borders with dots of icing.

AT THE RECEPTION: Position 14 in. plate on candlelight stand, add

dots of royal icing on plate and position 12 in. plate and 7 in. pillars. Arrange silk flowers; position cakes and add scrolls to bottom border of cake. Position extra flowers between scrolls with dots of icing. Insert color flow Claddagh in cake and position figurine+ and candles.

*Note: The top tier is often saved for the first anniversary. The number of servings given does not include the top tier.

+Warning: Always place a separator plate on the cake before you position any figurine or ornament. This protects both the cake and your keepsake. For extra stability, secure your figurine or ornament to the plate with tacky craft tape.

(For a complete product listing, see page 125.)

friendship, love, & loyalty

The Claddagh design hails from a tiny Irish fishing village, where it was displayed on boat sails to identify other friendly fishermen. Traditionally, two hands (friendship) hold a heart (love), topped by a crown (loyalty). We've adapted this beautiful design to crown our romantic candlelight cake—the perfect beginning to a journey of friendship, love and loyalty.

rose canopy

Even if your wedding will be small, you can still have a cake of grand proportions. It's fine to use "dummy" tiers in all sizes and configurations. Or, make a full-size cake, serving guests one piece at the reception and one to take home.

Cake Serves 327*
Features "With This Ring" Figurine and Push-in Pillar and Stacked Construction.

CAKE PREPARATION: For assembled tiers, make the following 2-layer round cakes: one 6 in., three 10 in. and two 14 in. The top tiers holding the staircases must be craft block dummies measuring 8 in. diameter x 4 in. high. Attach the dummies to 9 in. Crystal-Look Separator Plates with hot glue. For cakes surrounding the tiers, make eight 1-layer 6 in. round cakes. Prepare 2-layer cakes for push-in pillar and stacked construction (see page 107); prepare all cakes and craft block dummies for rolled fondant by lightly icing with buttercream; cover and smooth with Easy Glide Smoothers. Use Cake Dividing Set to divide 2-layer 6 in. and 8 in. tiers into 6ths, 10 in. cakes into 4ths.

On 8 in. dummies, imprint curlique pattern press at division marks 1 in. from cake bottom. Overpipe imprints with tip 16; add tip 2 dots above curliques. Repeat same process on 2-layer 6 in. cake. On 10 in. cakes, imprint scroll pattern press at division marks, 1 in. from bottom and 1 in. apart. Overpipe imprints with tip 16. Pipe tip 16 fleur de lis above each scroll and add tip 2 dots between scrolls. On all cakes, pipe tip 21 shell bottom borders.

(Instructions continued on page 40.)

(Instructions continued from page 38.)

Next, make fondant drapes for 1-layer 6 in. cakes. Fondant is easy to shape and position exactly the way you want. Roll out fondant and cut two 6 in. x 4 in. pieces for each cake. Gather pieces at ends, form a gentle drape. Brush back of garland with water and attach to side of cake. Pipe tip 21 rosette at beginning point of each drape and add tip 2 dots.

AT THE RECEPTION: Assemble cakes and stairway set. To secure and support stairs on the tops of 8 in. dummies, before reception, drill two holes in the bottom stair on each side; insert wooden dowel rods through the holes and into the dummy cakes. The stairs can still be reused at a later date.

Attach florist foam on stairs with florist tape and position fresh flowers on stairways. Also fill crystal bowls with florist foam, add fresh flowers and position between pillars. Place remaining fresh flowers in flower spikes and position on tops of 1-layer 6 in. cakes and at bottom border of 14 in. cakes. String ribbon through filigree bells and attach with glue gun under bridge. Position figurine.

*Note: The top tier is often saved for the first anniversary. The number of servings given does not include the top 6 in. tier.

ivory rose

Ivory roses fill a classic basketweave urn to create a beautiful bridal topiary. It's a lovely new way to top wedding cakes, while keeping a traditional look. The topiary also makes an elegant floral keepsake of the wedding day to display in your home.

Cake Serves 72*
Features "Ivory Rose" Topiary and Stacked Construction.

ADVANCE WORK: Make your flowers about 2 days in ahead using royal icing. You will need 144 tip 101s roses on tip 5 bases. Make extras to allow for breakage and let dry.

CAKE PREPARATION: Bake and cool 1-layer 6 in. round, 10 in. bevel top, 14 in. bevel bottom base and 2-layer 10 in. round cakes. Prepare cakes for stacked construction (see page 106). Prepare cakes for rolled fondant by lightly icing with buttercream. Cover cakes with fondant and smooth with Easy Glide Smoothers. Pipe tip 5 bead bottom borders.

Use Cake Dividing Set to divide 14 in. bottom bevel and 6 in. top round cakes into 8ths. Roll out fondant and cut eight 5³/4 in. x 3¹/2 in. drape pieces. Pinch ends of drapes together and attach to cake at division points with dots of icing.

Mold eight fondant urns using instructions on mold set. Unmold urns and attach with icing to cake sides, slightly above center of drape. Attach roses to top of urns and add tip 349 leaves. Attach 3 roses with dots of icing at each beginning point of drapes.

Add tip 349 leaves and tip 1 dots above roses.

On 6 in. cake, attach 3 roses at each division point; add tip 349 leaves. Add tip 1 dot garland between rose clusters 1³/8 in. from bottom edge; add more tip 1 dots below garland.

AT THE RECEPTION: Position topiary on separator plate.

(For a complete product listing, see page 125.)

ADVANCE WORK: Make flowers and leaves a few days ahead. Divide each of 2 packages of Ready-To-Use Fondant into thirds and tint as follows: 1/3 pk. rose, 1/3 pk. yellow, 1/3 pk. violet, 1/3 pk. peach, 2/3 pk. green. Using flower cutters and directions from the Flower Making Set, make the following flowers in rose, yellow, violet and peach: 144 large daisies (36 each color), 224 small daisies (56 each color), 224 wild roses (56 each color), 224 apple blossoms (56 each color), 144 pansies (36 each color). Dry on flower formers. Using green fondant, cutters and directions from Flower Making Set, make 100 small rose petals and 100 large rose leaves; emboss large rose leaves with leaf molds. Make extras of all flowers and leaves to allow for breakage. Let dry on flower formers.

When all flowers are completely dry, use royal icing to attach the following flowers: 36 apple blossoms inside same color large daisies; 18 wild roses inside same color pansies; 18 small daisies inside same color pansies. Pipe tip 3 royal icing white dot centers in flowers. Use tip 1 and green royal icing to pipe swirls in center of small rose petals.

CAKE PREPARATION: Bake and cool 2-layer 6 in., 10 in. and 14 in. cakes. Prepare for rolled fondant by lightly icing in buttercream. Prepare for plate and pillar construction (see page 107). Cover with fondant and smooth with Easy-Glide Fondant Smoothers.

To create sponge design on cake sides, thin green buttercream icing with a few drops of light corn syrup. Dip a crumpled paper towel in icing and "sponge" all around bottom 2 inches on all cakes. Randomly pipe tip 2 and tip 3 stems on cakes. Use royal icing to attach combination flowers to tip 3 stems and single flowers to tip 2 stems. Attach rose petals as leaves.

Pipe tip 5 bead bottom borders in green buttercream. While icing is still soft, tuck large rose leaves into bead border. Attach additional apple blossoms and small daisies around leaves with dots of icing. Pipe tip 2 zigzags around edges of square plates on cake tops. Assemble gazebo with hot glue gun and attach flowers and leaves with icing.

AT THE RECEPTION: Assemble cake, position gazebo and figurine+.

*Note: The top tier is often saved for the first anniversary. The number of servings given does not include the top tier.

+Warning: Always place a separator plate on the cake before you position any figurine or ornament. This protects both the cake and your keepsake. For extra stability, secure your ornament to the plate with tacky craft tape.

(For a complete product listing, see page 125.)

garden gala

Beautiful gardens and peaceful outdoor venues are highly sought after locations for today's weddings. Complete your garden theme with a lovely floral cake featuring the bridal couple sheltered in a charming gazebo. Use additional gazebos as centerpiece flower holders at each guest table.

exquisite lace

The bridal gown and flowers can inspire your wedding cake theme. A bride's veil or gown is often finished with breathtaking lace or embroidery. This can be echoed in a pattern to edge each cake layer. Look to the bride's bouquet to find a pretty flower to adorn each tier such as the gum paste orchids on this cake.

Cake Serves 164*
Features "Forevermore" Ornament and Push-in Pillar Construction.

ADVANCE WORK: Allow plenty of time for the shaping, drying and assembly of orchid bouquets. Make bouquets at least one week or more in advance. Remember, gum paste is sensitive to changes in temperature and humidity. Keep the climate in mind when making the recipe and when storing your finished flowers.

Using 2 cans of gum paste mix and cutters and instructions from Orchid Bouquet Flower Cutter Set, make 9 orchids, 40 stephanotis flowers, 35 stephanotis buds, and 125 ivy leaves. Make extras to allow for breakage and let dry. Use 12 in. lengths of florist wire covered with florist tape to make 35 tendrils. Wrap each tendril around decorator brush to form curls, then remove. You will make 9 bouquets, each including 1 orchid and 3 groupings of 1 stephanotis, 1 bud and 3 leaves. In each grouping, add a tendril folded in half to form a "V" and one pearl spray. The top bouquet uses no orchid and includes extra stephanotis. When orchids are dry, dust using a clean brush and grated non-toxic pastel chalk. Complete the bouquet assembly, adding extra leaves behind orchid.

To Make Lace Points: Copy enough Lace Point Patterns (see page 122) to make 80 pieces; tape to large cardboard or cake board. Cover pattern with waxed paper and lightly spray with vegetable pan spray for easy removal; wipe off excess spray with tissue. Outline with tip 2 and royal icing; make extras to allow for breakage and let dry.

CAKE PREPARATION: Bake and cool 2-layer 7, 10, 14 in. rounds and four 1-layer embossed hearts. Prepare cakes for rolled fondant by lightly icing with buttercream. Prepare for push-in pillar construction (see page 107). Cover cakes with fondant. Use Easy-Glide Smoothers on all cakes. Use Cake Dividing Set to divide 7 in. cake into 12ths, 10 in. cake into 16ths, 14 in. cake into 24ths (divide into 12ths, then divide each section in half).

For heart cakes, imprint Baby's Breath, Forget-Me-Not and Apple Blossom cutters from Floral Collection Set on cake. Use thinned royal icing and tip 2 to outline two largest flowers one at a time. Immediately pull icing into center of flower with a damp fine artist's brush. For smallest flowers use tip 1 and repeat same process as with tip 2. Add tip 2 dots and tip 5 bead bottom borders.

For 7, 10, 14 in. cakes, use largest and smallest rose petal cutter from Floral Collection Set to imprint pattern on sides of cake, 1/2 in. above bottom edge. Outline patterns one at a time with thinned royal icing and tip 2. Use damp fine artist's brush to pull icing into center of flowers. Add tip 2 dots to cake sides. Add tip 363 shell bottom border to 7 in. cake and tip 364 shell bottom borders to 10 and 14 in. cakes.

AT THE RECEPTION: Use hidden pillars cut to same height as heart cakes. Position craft block in center of table and position heart cakes around it. Position 16 in. plate on hearts, using hidden pillars for added support. Finish assembling cake. Position bouquet and ornament[+] on top tier. Pipe tip 4 line of icing on plate edges and gently position lace points. Position orchid bouquets.

[+]*Warning: Always place a separator plate on the cake before you position any figurine or ornament. This protects both the cake and your keepsake. For extra stability, secure your topper to the plate with tacky craft tape.*

*Note: The top tier is often saved for the first anniversary. The number of servings given does not include the top tier.

(For a complete product listing, see page 125.)

make it magical

Lighthearted and fun, Mickey and Minnie's cake is dazzling with magical fireworks, ribbon curls and enchanted colors! Look closely, each burst of fireworks is made of stars, hearts, roses and drop flowers—all symbolic of everlasting love.

Cake Serves 243*
Features "Mickey and Minnie in Love" Figurine and Push-In Pillar and Stacked Construction.

Note: Make this cake using pound cake to support the weight of the decorations.

ADVANCE WORK: Make royal icing decorations several days ahead. In white, make 700 tip 16 stars, 800 tip 131 drop flowers with tip 2 dot centers. In rose, make 450 tip 101 ribbon roses, 600 tip 5 hearts, 5 tip 8 hearts. In violet, make 800 tip 16 stars. Make extras of all to allow for breakage and let dry.

Next, assemble 20 fireworks: For each, stack twelve 18 in. lengths of 32 gauge white florist wire. Fold the stack of wire in half and twist floral tape around bottom to secure. Separate the wires and insert the folded end into a craft block to hold. Attach stars, drop flowers, ribbon roses and small hearts randomly to the wires using dots of royal icing. Attach the large hearts to the fireworks stack that will be positioned on top of the cake. Let dry at least one day.

CAKE PREPARA-TION: Bake and cool 2-layer 7, 10, 14 and 18 in. cakes. For the 18 in. Half Round, you'll need four cakes, stacked together to form one 2-layer cake. Ice smooth and prepare all tiers for push-in pillar and stacked construction. Dowel rod top tier for placement of figurine.

Now, decorate the tiers. Using butter-cream icing, pipe tip 21 star bottom

and tip 16 star top borders. Cut ribbon into 8 to 12 in. lengths and curl. On all tiers, attach ribbon on inside of the top borders by pushing one end of ribbon into icing. Attach remaining stars, ribbon roses, drop flowers and hearts to cake sides using dots of icing.

AT THE RECEPTION: First, place the fireworks in the flower spikes. These will be positioned evenly in the tiers; eight on the 18 in. tier, six on the 14 in. tier, five on the 10 in. tier, one on the 7 in. tier. Mark the positions on the tiers with dots of icing, then pipe tip 21 rosettes on the marks. Insert the spikes at the centers of the rosettes. Position the upper portion of the Petite Heart Base on the top tier and add figurine.[+] Add ribbon around base of cake.

[+]*Warning: Always place a separator plate on the cake before you position any figurine or ornament. This protects both the cake and your keepsake. For extra stability, secure your figurine or ornament to the plate with tacky craft tape.*

**The top tier is often saved for the first anniversary. The number of servings given does not include the top tier.*

(For a complete product listing, see page 125.)

©Disney

fabulous flavors

No longer does yellow cake reign—today a wedding cake can be a personal expression of the couple's tastes. Cheesecake and chocolate are always favorites, as in this cake which combines vanilla cheesecake and white chocolate bows. Serve each slice with a drizzle of raspberry or chocolate sauce.

Cake Serves 315*
Features Plate and Pillar Construction.

ADVANCE WORK: The bows on our cheesecakes are assembled from 12 or 13 individual candy loops and are attached to candy bases made in our Muffin Caps Pan. Prepare ribbon loops and bases at least 1 to 2 weeks in advance.

To make ribbons, cut 230 strips of freezer paper 1 in. wide x 7 in. long. In order to create the curve of the loop, be sure to cut the 7 in. length in the natural curving direction of the freezer paper roll. Pour melted candy into a cut disposable decorating bag and squeeze onto the glossy side of freezer paper strips. Cover entire strip and smooth with a small angled spatula. Lift pieces and clean edges with fingertips. Set aside for 1 to 1½ minutes until candy just begins to firm. Press ends together to form loop and rest on side to let completely dry. (Make extras to allow for breakage.)

To make 16 bases for ribbon bows, fill Muffin Caps cavities halfway with melted candy. Refrigerate until firm. (Make extras to allow for breakage.)

To assemble loops, position candy base on 6 in. cake board covered with waxed paper. (Note: The cake board

will serve as a guide to help you center loops of bows and give you an idea of how it will look on cake.) Remove paper from loops; attach 6 loops with melted candy for bow bottom and fill in spaces with 6-7 more to complete bow. Let set.

CAKE PREPARATION: Following recipe on page 117, make seven 6 x 3 in. and nine 8 x 3 in. cheesecakes. Note: Place a cake board in bottom of springform pans before assembling and baking cheesecake. This will make it easier to remove cakes and the springform bottom will be ready to use for the next cake. Bake and cool cakes. Using buttercream icing, pipe tip 366 leaf bottom border on all cakes.

AT THE RECEPTION: Position 3 in. pillars between two 18 in. plates; add roman columns and two 6 in. plates. Position 6 in. cakes on top and on 18 in. plate. Add surrounding 8 in. cakes. Position bows on cakes. Add fresh flowers.

*Note: The top tier is often saved for the first anniversary. The number of servings given does not include the top tier.

(For a complete product listing, see page 125.)

CAKE PREPARATION: Bake and cool 2-layer 8 in., 12 in. and 16 in. cakes. Ice smooth and prepare for plate and pillar construction (see page 107).

On 8 in. tier: Mark each side of cake into 8 equal divisions, 1 in. apart. Pipe rows of tip 6 upright beads at division marks. Pipe tip 1 sotas on cake top and over sides. Pipe tip 6 bead bottom border.

On 12 in. tier: Mark each side of cake into 10 equal divisions, 1 1/4 in. apart. Position 9 in. square separator plate on cake top, toward back corner. Pipe rows of tip 21 upright shells at division marks. Pipe tip 1 sotas on cake top and over sides. Pipe tip 21 shell bottom border. Pipe tip 6 line around separator plate scallops.

On 16 in. tier: Mark each side of cake into 16 equal divisions, 1 in. apart. Position 13 in. separator plate on cake top, toward back corner. Pipe alternating rows of tip 6 beads and tip 21 shells at division marks. Pipe tip 1 sotas on cake top and over sides. Pipe tip 21 shell bottom border. Pipe tip 6 line around separator plate scallops.

AT THE RECEPTION: Assemble cake; add fresh flowers and position ornament.[+]

Warning: Always place a separator plate on the cake before you position any figurine or ornament. This protects both the cake and your keepsake. For extra stability, secure your topper to the plate with tacky craft tape.

*Note: The top tier is often saved for the first anniversary. The number of servings given does not include the top tier.

(For a complete product listing, see page 125.)

ivory
inspiration

Even as new options emerge in bridal fashion, brides continue to match their cake to their gown. The traditional color for the wedding cake has been white like the bridal gown. With today's new fabrics and the desire of brides to look their very best, warm hues of ivory, off white and cream are coming down the aisle—and appearing on the cake.

ADVANCE WORK: Use royal icing and flower nail #9 to make 44 tip 101s white carnations with tip 3 bases and 36 tip 104 rose colored carnations with tip 10 bases. Make extras to allow for breakage and let dry.

CAKE PREPARATION: Bake and cool 2-layer 9¼ and 12½ in. cakes. Ice smooth and prepare for stacked construction (see page 106). Pipe tip 48 basketweave on sides of both cakes. Pipe tip 127D ruffle bottom border on 12½ in. heart cake. Position carnations around top borders and at top of ruffle. Add tip 352 leaves. At the reception, position ornament.[+]

"Heart Adoration"
Serves 124*
Features *"Our First Dance"* Ornament and Stacked Construction.

ADVANCE WORK: Make the fondant bows and flowers. For bows, use one package of fondant rolled out about ⅛ in. thick. Cut 11 strips, 1 in. x 6 in.; reserve remaining fondant. Fold these strips in half to form bows;

attach with a damp brush. Roll a small ball of fondant for each bow and position at center. For flowers and leaves, use 1 package fondant; tint ¼ light rose, ¼ dark rose, ¼ green, leave ¼ white. Roll out fondant ⅛ in. thick and use flower ejector to cut approximately 360 small flowers—120 each in light rose, dark rose and white. Add tip 1 dot centers to each. Use leaf cutter from ejector set to make 150 green leaves. Make extras of all to allow for breakage and let dry.

CAKE PREPARATION: Bake and cool 2-layer 9¼ in., 12½ in. and 14¼ in. cakes. Ice smooth with white buttercream icing; use pink buttercream for sides of 14¼ in. cake. Prepare cakes for stacked construction (see page 106). Divide top tier into eleven 3-inch divisions; middle tier into twelve 4-inch divisions; bottom tier into eleven 4⅛-inch divisions.

On bottom tier, use largest nesting heart cookie cutter and reserved white fondant to cut out 11 hearts; immediately position one at each division point; edge each with tip 5 beads.

Attach flower clusters and leaves to heart centers with tip 2 dots of icing. Pipe tip 1 vines around flowers. Pipe tip 12 heart bottom border; position flower at center of each heart.

On top and middle tiers, use tip 1 to pipe curlique lines on cake tops and sides. Between division points, position flowers in garland formation and add leaves. Add tip 5 bead bottom border on both cakes. On middle cake attach bows and white fondant flowers between bows.

AT THE RECEPTION: Raise the cake off the table using a board about 1 in. thick (the board should be slightly smaller in diameter than the base cake). Arrange baby's breath and position ornament.[+]

[+]*Warning: Always place a separator plate on the cake before you position any figurine or ornament. This protects both the cake and your keepsake. For extra stability, secure your topper to the plate with tacky craft tape.*

**Note: The top tier is often saved for the first anniversary. The number of servings given does not include the top tier.*

(For a complete product listing, see page 125.)

heart to heart

Including hearts at your wedding is as traditional as playing "The Wedding March". Not just a symbol of love—the heart tells us we are in love and measures the excitement we feel on the wedding day. Make your heart cake romantic or lighthearted with your choice of accents and ornament.

lavish cascades

Pure romance will never go out of fashion. The English Lambeth style of cake design lends itself very well to richly decorated settings such as hotel receptions. Lambeth decorating features cascading bands lush with overpiped curves and scrolls which give the cake breathtaking dimension.

Cake Serves 153*
Features "Only the Beginning" Figurine and Pillar and Stacked Construction.

ADVANCE WORK: At least 1 week ahead, use royal icing to make trim and flowers. Using tip 127 and the 2^{1}/$_{2}$ in. lily nail, make 16 petunias. Pipe tip 17 star centers and add 10 stamens to each center. Make 90 tip 66 bluebells with tip 3 dot centers using the 1^{1}/$_{4}$ in. lily nail. Add 3 pearl stamens to each center. Also pipe 200 tip 224 drop flowers with tip 3 dot centers. To make large scrolls: Using the pattern (see page 122), make 32 tip 32 scrolls. Let dry and attach 2 scrolls back to back, using royal icing to secure, let dry. Next, the scrolls will be overpiped in a Lambeth style. To avoid the decorations shifting or collapsing from the weight of the moist icing, pipe one row at a time and allow icing to dry between steps. Pipe tip 18 zigzag along the outside seam of the scroll. Add tip 18 straight line over the zigzag; overpipe center of scroll with tip 5 then tip 3 lines. To make bands: Cover the outsides of large flower formers with waxed paper. Tape in place. Pipe 32 tip 2B bands (smooth side up) over the formers. Let dry. On 16 of the bands, overpipe with tip 18 zigzag, tip 18 line, then tip 5 and tip 3 lines. On the other 16 bands, attach bluebells with dots of icing.

Cover the outsides of medium flower formers with waxed paper and pipe 56 tip 2B bands (serrated side up). On 8 of the bands, add tip 18 zigzags and position drop flowers. The remaining 48 bands remain undecorated. Make extras of all decorations to allow for breakage and let dry completely.

CAKE PREPARATION: Bake and cool 1-layer 18 in. half round (you'll need two cakes, positioned to form one full round layer, 3 in. high), 1-layer 12 in. round (3 in. high), 3-layer 8 in. round (to measure 5 in. high) and ^{1}/$_{2}$ ball cake. Ice smooth in buttercream icing and prepare all tiers for pillar and stacked construction (see page 108). Using the Cake Dividing Set, mark round tiers into 16ths, marking 1^{3}/$_{4}$ in. down from the top edge. Divide the ^{1}/$_{2}$ ball cake into 8ths, marking 2 in. up from bottom.

Decorate ^{1}/$_{2}$ ball cake: Position large gumball on top, add bands with drop flowers at marks. Attach bluebells on top of gumball with dots of icing. Next, pipe tip 3 double drop strings, add tip 3 dots at point. Pipe tip 18 shell bottom border. Add drop flowers between shells. Decorate 8 in.

tier: Pipe tip 16 scallop around plate. Pipe tip 32 crown border, add tip 18 straight line over shell and overpipe with tip 5 then tip 3 lines. Make sure each line piped attaches to cake when you start to pipe—after you bring the line over the shell, attach to the side of the cake. Allow icing to dry between steps. Pipe tip 3 drop string between each shell, add dots to points. Pipe tip 16 zigzag garland, ^{3}/$_{4}$ in. deep between marks. Add tip 3 drop strings over garland and ^{1}/$_{4}$ and ^{1}/$_{2}$ in. below. Position drop flowers at garland points. Pipe tip 32 shell bottom border. Decorate 12 in. tier: Pipe tip 16 zigzag garland at marks and add tip 3 double drop strings. Pipe tip 32 shell bottom border. Decorate 18 in. tier: Pipe tip 4B shell bottom border. Position bands (from the medium flower formers) on the bottom border centered between the marks. Place a petunia on each band, gently pushing back of flower into bottom border.

AT THE RECEPTION: Assemble top tier on pillars. Attach remaining bands to cake with dots of icing as follows: On 12 in. tier, position large scrolls over edge of cake resting on top of 18 in. tier. Place the bands with bluebells in between the large scrolls. On the 18 in. tier, position bands (from large flower formers) in between the petunias. Add two bands (from medium flower formers) above each petunia, on each side of the large scrolls on the 12 in. tier; trim the bottom of each band with a drop flower. Position figurine between pillars.

*Note: The top tier is often saved for the first anniversary. The number of servings given does not include the top tier.

(For a complete product listing, see page 126.)

butterflies

The butterfly symbolizes transformation—reaching a higher level of beauty and spirit. Isn't that what weddings are all about? That's why butterflies are often released to greet the newlyweds (much more elegant than rice!) and are turning up on everything from bridal accessories to invitations. And now, butterflies arrive on cakes and matching cupcakes, dotted with daisies and flowing with ribbon.

"Floating On Air" Serves 100*
Features Floating Tiers Cake Stand Set.

ADVANCE WORK: Make flowers about 2 or 3 weeks in advance, using rolled fondant.

You will need 500 small daisies, 250 large daisies and 55 daisies on wires. This number of flowers will also give you enough to make the cupcakes shown here. Make extra flowers to allow for breakage, and let dry following instructions.

Next, make a double-tied bow with streamers. You'll need about 1 1/2 yards of 1 in. wide white ribbon with wired edges for flexibility. Set the bow aside.

CAKE PREPARATION: Bake and cool 2-layer 9 in., 12 in. and 15 in. petal cakes, then ice smooth. Pipe tip 4 bead top and bottom borders. Starting from the petal points (the indentations on the cake sides), pipe double drop strings using tip 13. Strings should measure 2 3/4 in. and

2 1/4 in. from the bottom of the cake. Attach daisies to sides of cake with dots of icing.

Next, make a daisy bouquet: Using florist wire, wrap together about 25 daisies on wires and 2 butterflies. To hold the bouquet, you will core the center of your top 9 in. cake. Do this with a "Hidden" Pillar—just push the pillar straight down into the center of the cake and lift up to remove a cylinder of cake. After cleaning, position the pillar in the cored area and place the bouquet inside.

AT THE RECEPTION: Attach bow to bouquet with dots of icing. Position additional daisies and butterflies on cake centers.

"Butterfly Cupcakes"
CAKE PREPARATION: Bake, cool, and ice 2 dozen cupcakes smooth. Position large and small daisies on each cupcake. Prepare daisy bouquet following instructions for the butterfly cake.

AT THE RECEPTION: Assemble Tall Tier Cake Stand, glue legs onto the 14 in. plate and place cupcakes on plates. Attach top cap nut for stability. Next, add daisy bouquet. Position bouquet in the hole on top cap nut. Attach additional daisies to plates and columns using icing.

*Note: The top tier is often saved for the first anniversary. The number of servings given does not include the top tier.

(For a complete product listing, see page 126)

joyous
rainbow

Today there is no limit to color—so why not introduce a rainbow as your wedding theme? Many colors can be used on the cake as well as the flowers. Accent the reception using ribbon bows and candies in all the colors to add a festive touch.

Cake Serves 195*
Features "Ethnic Love's Duet" Figurine and Romantic Heart Base with Pillar Construction.

ADVANCE WORK: Make the following fondant decorations at least one week ahead. Make 100 pastel curls in each color—Golden Yellow, Rose, Violet and Kelly Green. For each color, combine one box Ready-To-Use Rolled Fondant with 1/2 can prepared gum paste. First, tint the mixture very pale Golden Yellow, then add each color to that mixture to produce a light pastel. Roll out fondant 1/8 in. thick, and cut into 1 in. x 8 in. long strips. Roll the strips and stand on end to dry on cornstarch-dusted waxed paper.

Using white fondant, make ball decorations. If fondant feels too soft, add confectioners' sugar to firm. You will need six balls 11/4 in. diameter, 12 balls 1 in. diameter, 12 balls 3/4 in. diameter and 260 balls 1/2 in. diameter. Dry on waxed paper dusted with cornstarch.

CAKE PREPARATION: Bake and cool 2-layer 8, 10, 12 and 16 in. tiers.

Ice smooth and prepare for pillar construction. Divide all tiers into sixths using the Cake Dividing Set. Mark garlands on cake sides between division marks. For the 12, 10 and 8 in. tiers, mark 13/4 in. from the bottom border. On the 16 in. tier, mark 1 in. from the top border at division marks. Pipe a tip 8 ball bottom border on all tiers using buttercream icing. Roll white fondant 1/8 in. thick and cut into strips 3/4 in. wide x 8 in. long. Lay strips in a ribbon fashion on bottom borders.

Attach fondant balls to garland marks on cake sides using dots of icing. Use the 1/2 in. balls on the 8, 10 and 12 in. tiers. On the 16 in. tier, place the largest (11/4 in.) ball at the bottom border, centered between division marks. Then position 1 in. balls on each side, followed by 3/4 in. balls. Fill in the remaining garland with 1/2 in. balls.

Attach curls along top edges of all tiers with dots of icing. Loosely lay curls on cake tops. On top tier,

position base on top, then add curls around it.

AT THE RECEPTION: Position tiers on pillars. Place figurine on top tier.[+]

*Note: The top tier is often saved for the first anniversary. The number of servings given does not include the top tier.

[+]Warning: Always place a separator plate on the cake before you position any figurine or ornament. This protects both the cake and your keepsake. For extra stability, secure your figurine or ornament to the plate with tacky craft tape.

(For a complete product listing, see page 126.)

blossoms of love

A small cake can look large or a large cake can look larger by using more than one separation between cake layers. Fountains or mini accents can fill out the cake, giving you a design that matches the size of your dreams without adding more cake than guests.

Cake Serves 139*
Features "Reflections" Ornament and "Happiness Ribbon" Tier Top and Pillar and Stacked Construction.

ADVANCE WORK: Make petunias several days in advance using stiff consistency royal icing and lily nails lined with foil. Make 30 large petunias using tips 103 and 16 with the $1^5/8$ in. lily nail; add white stamens to centers. Make 80 small petunias using tips 102 and 16 with the $1^1/4$ in. lily nail, add white stamens to centers. Make extras to allow for breakage and let dry in foil.

The royal icing swags for the 16 in. tier should also be made several days in advance. Cover the sides of the 16 in. round pan with waxed paper—this will be your work surface. Using the Cake Dividing Set, divide sides into 12ths. With very stiff royal icing and tip 127, pipe swags, $1^1/2$ in. deep, from each division point. Make only 6 swags at one time, you will need a

total of 12. Make extras to allow for breakage and let dry.

CAKE PREPARATION: Bake and cool 2-layer 7 in., 10 in. and 16 in. cakes. Ice smooth and prepare for pillar and stacked construction (see page 108). Cover 7 in. cake completely with tip 1 sotas. On 10 in. cake, pipe tip 127 ruffle bottom border; add tip 1 sotas on top of ruffle and edge with tip 3 beads.

Position 11 in. plate on top of 16 in. cake; edge with tip 5 beads. Using Cake Dividing Set, divide cake into 12ths. Attach dried swags, $1^1/2$ in. from top, on cake sides at division points. Pipe tip 1 sotas on top and sides of cake. Pipe tip 127 ruffle bottom border; add tip 1 sotas on top of ruffle and edge with tip 3 beads.

Attach small and large petunias on top of 10 in. cake. Position leaves. Pipe tip 3 tendrils on sides of 10 in. cake.

AT THE RECEPTION: Attach petunias inside swags; attach leaves. Add ornament[+] and tier top. Position fountain and cascade; add fresh flowers to flower holder ring.

[+]*Warning: Always place a separator plate on the cake before you position any figurine or ornament. This protects both the cake and your keepsake. For extra stability, secure your topper to the plate with tacky craft tape.*

*Note: The top tier is often saved for the first anniversary. The number of servings given does not include the top tier.

(For a complete product listing, see page 126.)

bride & groom

Pattern your wedding cake after your own image. Personalize the bride and groom cake simply by adapting hair color and other distinguishing features. This cake gives your reception and cake cutting ceremony a wonderful lighthearted touch.

Cakes Serve 263*
Features "Mini Wedding Couple" Figurine with Push-In Pillar and Stacked Construction.

WEDDING CAKE (Serves 9.):
ADVANCE WORK: Use royal icing and Flower Nail No. 7 to make approximately 28 tip 102 pink roses with tip 7 bases. Make extras to allow for breakage and let dry.

CAKE PREPARATION: Bake and cool 2-layer 4 in. Springform and 1-layer 6 in. round cakes. Ice smooth and prepare for push-in pillar construction (see page 107). Using the Cake Dividing Set, mark 4 in. tier into 6ths and 6 in. tier into 8ths. Pipe tip 16 zigzag garland between marks on both tiers. Pipe tip 16 shell top and bottom borders; add shells around pillars. Position roses at bottom borders alternating with tip 352 leaves.

AT THE RECEPTION: Assemble tier on pillars. Pipe tip 16 shells around pillars. Position Mini Wedding Couple Figurine.

BRIDE CAKE (Serves 120):
ADVANCE WORK: Use royal icing and Flower Nail No. 7 to make 7 tip 104 pink roses with tip 12 bases. Make 1 tip 104 pink rosebud with tip

3 green sepals and stem; set this aside for the groom. Make extras to allow for breakage and let dry.

CAKE PREPARATION: Bake and cool 2-layer 8 in., 1-layer 10 in. (3 in. high), 1-layer 12 in. (3 in. high) cakes. Prepare for rolled fondant and stacked construction (see page 106). The 10 in. and 12 in. tiers will need 3 packages of white fondant total. The 8 in. tier will need 1 package of white fondant tinted copper (lt. skintone). Cover the cakes following package instructions.

Cut copper fondant neckline 4 in. wide x 3 in. deep. Cut other fondant decorations using patterns (see page 119) and a sharp knife. Tint a small amount of fondant pink and cut lips; cut 2 cheeks using large end of tip 1A. Form nose from copper fondant. Cut eyes: 2 whites using large end of tip 126; 2 black pupils using large end of tip 12. Attach these fondant pieces using damp brush.

Measure a length of pearl beading around the neck. Cut off length and

attach, securing with damp brush at the back. Decorate the following using buttercream icing: Pipe tip 32 rosettes for hair; position floral spray headpiece. Add tip 2 eyelashes. Cover dress with tip 2 cornelli lace. Edge neckline with tip 16 zigzags. Position roses and ribbon for bouquet, add tip 352 leaves. Pipe tip 32 shell bottom border, top with tip 127D ruffle. Edge ruffle with tip 16 zigzag garland. Gather tulle for veil and attach to top of head using dots of icing.

GROOM CAKE (Serves 134):
CAKE PREPARATION: Bake and cool 2-layer 6 in., 2-layer 8 in., 1-layer 10 in. (3 in. high), 1-layer 12 in. (3 in. high) cakes. Prepare for rolled fondant by lightly icing with buttercream. Prepare for stacked construction (see page 106). Tint 5 packages of chocolate fondant black and cover 10 in. and 12 in. tiers, 6 in. tier and an 8 in. cake circle. The 8 in. tier needs 1 package of white fondant tinted copper (lt. skintone). Assemble the top hat by attaching the 6 in. tier to the cake circle using icing.

Using patterns (see page 119) and black fondant, cut a right lapel, left lapel and bow tie. Cut white tuxedo front using pattern. Tint a small amount of fondant pink and cut 2 cheeks using large end of tip 1A. Form nose and 2 ears from copper fondant. Cut eyes: 2 whites using large end of tip 126; 2 black pupils using large end of tip 12. Roll a string of black fondant and form for mouth; cut 2 black buttons using small end of tip 1A. Attach these fondant pieces to groom using damp brush. Using buttercream icing, pipe tip 16 string hair and overpipe for dimension. Attach rosebud to lapel with a dot of icing.

*Note: The number of servings does not include the top layer of the two-tier "wedding cake".

(For a complete product listing, see page 126.)

faith
&
devotion

Express your faith and devotion with an inspirational theme cake. Use lush arrangements of pure white roses and soft candlelight to set a sacred and uplifting tone for the day.

Cake Serves 72*
Features "Inspirational Cross" Figurine and Stacked Construction.

CAKE PREPARATION: Bake and cool 2-layer 12 and 15 in. hexagon cakes. Ice smooth and prepare for stacked construction (see page 106). Add tip 2 cornelli lace on tops and sides. Pipe tip 5 bead bottom borders on both cakes. Gather tulle circles into puffs. Set aside.

AT THE RECEPTION: Position separator ring on separator plate.

Position Floral Figurine Pedestal and Cross. Place floral oasis in Fresh Flower Holders at bottom of base cake; arrange fresh flowers and approximately 60 tulle puffs around cakes.

*Note: The top tier is often saved for the first anniversary. The number of servings given does not include the top tier.

(For a complete product listing, see page 126.)

"Vibrant Blooms" Serves 14*

ADVANCE WORK: Make fondant/gum paste blossoms and bee at least 1 to 2 weeks in advance. To make blossoms, see pages 116 and 117. Make extras to allow for breakage.

To make fondant bee: roll out 1 in. long x $1/2$ in. high body using yellow fondant; add small black stripes. Roll small ball of black fondant and flatten for head; add white dot eyes and black dot pupils, attach with water. Cover toothpick with black fondant and insert in back of bee for stinger. Cut wings and attach. Insert florist wire and let dry in craft block.

CAKE PREPARATION: Bake and cool 10 in. ring mold cake. Add 5 tablespoons of corn syrup to each 3 cups of buttercream icing to thin. Ice cake smooth and use spatula to create vertical stripes on cake sides. Divide cake into 8ths. Tint $1/2$ package of rolled fondant light yellow. Roll out and cut eight $1/2$ in. x 8 in. strips.

Ruffle edges of strips with sharpened dowel rod. Pipe tip 5 bead bottom border. Position ruffled fondant strips on cake sides at division points, tapering toward bottom border of cake. Roll $3/4$ in. balls of white fondant and position around bottom border of cake. Pipe tip 2 swirls on ball bottom border.

To make tulle puffs, gather $31/2$ x $31/2$ in. tulle squares and tie with florist wire. Cover florist wire with floral tape. Cut craft block 4 in. round x 3 in. high and cover with Fanci-Foil. Position in center of cake.

AT THE RECEPTION: Insert flowers**, tulle puffs and bee into block. Position 16 side blossoms with icing.

Note: On the centerpiece cakes, the entire cake is served.

**PLEASE NOTE: FLOWERS INSERTED IN CENTER OF CAKE ARE NOT EDIBLE.*

(For a complete product listing, see page 126.)

"Season of Love" Serves 30*
Features Plate and Pillar Construction

ADVANCE WORK: Use royal icing and flower nail No. 7 to make 117 tip 101s zinnias (see page 115). Make extras to allow for breakage and let dry.

CAKE PREPARATION: Bake and cool 2-layer 8 in. round cakes and three Singles!™ 4 in. springform cakes. Ice smooth, sides yellow and tops white. Prepare for plate and pillar construction (see page 107). Pipe tip 7 bead top and bottom borders. Position zinnias on top and bottom borders and around center of cake.

AT THE RECEPTION: Assemble cake and position fresh flowers using crystal-look bowl on bottom, and crystal-look base on top. Position center flowers on separator plate.

Note: On centerpiece cakes, the entire cake is served. Servings include both tiers of this cake.

(For a complete product listing, see page 123.)

Bring the beauty of the wedding cake to each guest table. Centerpiece cakes are a festive decorating touch that will help your guests feel part of the celebration. Ask your caterer to have each cake cut and served right at the table.

centerpiece cakes

wildest dreams

With the new freedom in wedding cake design, you can combine different shapes and colors to create a truly distinctive look. This cake has it all—classic garlands, contemporary twists and cool pastels—for a fun design that expresses today's more carefree attitude.

Cake Serves 233
Features "Classic Couple" Figurine and Push-In Pillar and Stacked Construction.

ADVANCE WORK: Color the fondant, tinting 3 packages light Kelly Green, 7 packages Royal Blue, 3 packages Violet with Rose added. Reserve 1 package White.

Two days ahead, make 18 fondant stars using the 2 smallest stars of the nesting cutter set. Roll out fondant 1/4 in. thick, and cut 3 stars of each size and color. Roll 3/8 in. diameter ropes of matching color fondant. Brush lollipop stick with water and twist rope onto sticks. Dry on waxed paper dusted with cornstarch. Use a 1/4 in. ball of fondant, brushed with water, to attach star to stick. Let dry.

CAKE PREPARATION: Bake and cool 2-layer 18 in. and 8 in. and 1-layer 8 in. and 6 in. cakes. Prepare for fondant by lightly covering with buttercream icing. (2-layer 12 in. will be completed later). Cover with tinted fondant. Prepare for push-in pillar and stacked construction (page 107).
Decorate 18 in. 2-layer tier: Roll fondant into 5/8 in. thick rope; you will need 6 ropes, each 20 in. long. Twist 2 ropes together and attach to bottom with water. Repeat with remaining rope sections. Using Cake Dividing Set, mark tier into 10ths. For each garland, cut fondant 6 in. long x 4 1/2 in. deep. Gather sides, shape, trim excess with scissors. Brush back with water and attach to cake sides between marks. Make 10

teardrop bases 2 1/2 in. long and attach with water to cake at each division. Make 10 tassels, one at a time to prevent drying out (see page 116). Attach at each division. Place 9 in. separator plate 1/2 in. from right edge of 18 in. cake. Place a 6 in. cake circle directly to the left of the plate, mark area. Next, remove plate and circle and dowel rod that area of cake. Position the 12 in. cake circle over the left side of the separator plate and covering the 6 in. circle. Mark the 12 in. cake circle for feet and cut out placement openings. Remove 12 in. cake circle. Prepare 12 in. cake for fondant covering. Cover with tinted fondant. Divide the tier into 12ths and mark center of tier. Position this tier on the 18 in. tier, aligning cut out areas on board with feet of separator plate.
Decorate 12 in. 2-layer tier: Cut twelve 1 in. wide x 9 in. long strips of fondant. Brush with water and attach to cake at division marks. Work from the bottom border up, trim off excess. Using pattern (see page 122), cut diamonds from fondant and attach with water to strips beginning 1 in. above bottom. Roll fondant into 3/4 in. balls, brush with water and attach to bottom border. Dowel rod the area where 8 in. tier will be positioned.
Decorate 8 in. 1-layer tier: Position tier to the right side of 12 in. tier. Imprint feet of 9 in. plate on cake top for placement of pillars,

aligning with the plate below. Make 25 ribbon roses: Cut fondant into strips 3/4 in. wide x 4 in. long. Roll, pinch bottom to secure and trim excess off bottom. Roll out fondant and cut 16 dots using large opening of any tip. Brush roses and dots with water and attach to cake. Roll one 3/4 in. diameter rope in violet and one 1/4 in. diameter rope in white, each 25 in. long. Loosely wrap the 1/4 in. rope around the 3/4 in. rope and attach to bottom with water. Insert hidden pillars at marks. Cover base of pillars with 1/4 in. rope.
Decorate 8 in. 2-layer tier: Divide tier into 12ths and position on 9 in. plate. Imprint cake top with 7 in. plate for placement of pillars. Cut fondant into 8 in. long x 3/4 in. wide strips. Twist, and attach to cake with water. Trim edges, do not overlap strips on cake top. Make 38 small puffs for bottom border and three large puffs for top of cake (see page 116). Insert 9 in. Disposable Pillars (without rings) into tier at marks. Roll 1/4 in. diameter rope and cover base of pillars.
Decorate 6 in. 1-layer tier: Cut 32 blue fondant stars using smallest cutter. Brush with water and position.

AT THE RECEPTION: Insert star sticks into cake top. Assemble tiers on pillars. Position figurine on cake top.

Note: Keep fondant cakes and decorations covered until reception to prevent fading.
(For a complete product listing, see page 127.)

something new, something blue

There are no boundaries to the shape and design of a wedding cake. This cake shape, which places the largest tier in the center, will certainly be the center of attention at the reception. The cake is decorated with blue morning glories, a great flower for morning or afternoon weddings. Select other flowers to match a theme for evening weddings.

Cake Serves 124**
Features "Pearl Essence" Ornament and Stacked and Center Column Construction.

ADVANCE WORK: Make the bridges which will hold flowers at least one week prior to decorating. Cover cake board with waxed paper; use royal icing and tip 1D (serrated side up) to pipe bands in the following lengths: eight 2^1/$_2$ in.; five 3 in.; eight 3^1/$_2$ in. and five 4 in. Make extras to allow for breakage and let dry.

At least 1 to 2 weeks in advance, use royal icing to make 120 tip 103 morning glories on 1^5/$_8$ in. lily nail and 200 tip 102 morning glories on 1^1/$_4$ in. lily nail (see *Decorating Cakes* book, page 67). Note: Violet and Royal Blue were combined to achieve color used for morning glories. Add tip 1 white lines in center and tip 2 yellow stamens to all. Make extras to allow for breakage and let dry.

CAKE PREPARATION: Bake and cool three 8 x 3 in. cakes; two 12 x 2 in. cakes and one 14 x 2 in.

cake. Prepare for stacked and center column construction, with an 8 in. cake on top of the 12 in. and 14 in. cakes (see page 109). Top tier must be decorated on foil-covered board and assembled at reception. Ice 8 in. cakes and use decorating comb on sides. Ice 12 in. and 14 in. cakes smooth. Divide 12 in. cakes into 8ths and 14 in. cake into 10ths. Pipe tip 17 shell top and bottom borders on 8 in. cakes.

AT THE RECEPTION: Assemble cakes following center column instructions. On top plate, secure columns with cap nut bolt. Position cake on top. Attach royal icing bridge pieces at division marks on cake sides: On 12 in. cakes, alternately position 2^1/$_2$ in. and 3^1/$_2$ in. bridges; on 14 in. cake, alternately position 3 in. and 4 in. bridges. Add tip 102 flowers to bridges with tip 2 dots of royal icing. Attach tip 102 flowers to ornament. Add tip 352

leaves. Attach 3^3/$_4$ in. and 4^1/$_2$ in. long strands of pearl beading* between bridges. Attach tip 102 and 103 flowers at bases of cakes. Add tip 352 leaves. Position ornament.[+]

Remove pearl beading before cutting and serving.

**Note: The top tier is often saved for the first anniversary. The number of servings given does not include one 8 in. tier.*

[+]*Warning: Always place a separator plate on the cake before you position any figurine or ornament. This protects both the cake and your keepsake. For extra stability, secure your topper to the plate with tacky craft tape.*

(For a complete product listing, see page 127.)

groom's
cakes

Believe it or not, before the 19th century, British couples actually wanted fruitcakes for their weddings. Good sense took over and lighter cakes gained favor, but the fruitcake was still served as a "groom's cake" to appeal to guests with different tastes. When the groom's cake tradition moved to America, fruitcake was again set aside in favor of luscious chocolate creations like those on the next four pages.

"Sweet Swirls" Serves 78*
Features Push-In Pillar Construction.

ADVANCE WORK: Make chocolate candy swirls several days ahead. Cover swirl pattern (see page 122) with waxed paper. Using melted candy in bag fitted with tip 4, outline 20 swirl pieces. Make extras to allow for breakage and set aside until firm. Turn firm chocolate pieces over and pipe once again with tip 4 and melted chocolate. Set aside until firm.

CAKE PREPARATION: Bake and cool 1-layer 6 in., 10 in. and 14 in. tiers, 3 in. high. Ice smooth. Prepare for push-in pillar construction (see

page 107). Position cakes on boards and crystal-look plates. Pipe tip 32 shell bottom border on all tiers; position Candy Melts® wafer between each shell. Pour melted canned fudge icing and position strawberries on cake tops; let excess icing drip down cake sides.

AT THE RECEPTION: Assemble cake. Insert chocolate swirl pieces in cakes, resting on berries.

*Note: Servings include all tiers of this cake.
(For a complete product listing, see page 127.)

Dessert Chocolates
Adding homemade candies to your sweet table is an easy way to serve guests something special. Make all candies using melted Dark or Light Cocoa Premium Candy Melts®. Prepare cordial cups following instructions on mold package. Make truffles using recipe in the *Wilton Candy Easy As 1-2-3 Book*, p. 35 or in *Wilton Yearbook of Cake Decorating*. Drizzle melted candy over truffles using a cut parchment bag. Dust some candy with cocoa powder, roll others in nuts and Sprinkles. Dip clean, dry strawberries in melted candy, let dry on waxed paper. Arrange on platters and serve. If desired, cordial cups can be filled with liqueur before serving.

(For a complete product listing, see page 127.)

"Bold Vision" Serves 81*
Features Stacked Construction.

ADVANCE WORK: Make the chocolate loops 1 week in advance to ensure proper drying time.

Mix 1 can of gum paste following package directions; let set 15 minutes and add brown icing color. Add 1 package of chocolate fondant to gum paste and knead together until combined. Repeat process with second can of gum paste and fondant. Roll out and cut 30 loops measuring 14 in. long x 1 in. wide; fold in half and let dry on sides. Cut 9 streamers 7 in. long x 1 in. wide; bend, twist and let dry on sides. Cut 15 curly streamers 1/2 in. wide x 10 in. long, twist, bend and let dry on sides. Make extras of all pieces to allow for breakage; dry for several days.

When completely dry, melt Candy Melts® and use tapered spatula to swirl on inside and outside of all loops and streamers. Let dry. Melt additional candy in disposable bag; cut bag tip and pipe beads around outside edges of loops and streamers. Let dry and set aside.

CAKE PREPARATION: Bake and cool 2-layer 8 in. and 12 in. cakes. Prepare for stacked construction (see page 106). Prepare for fondant by lightly icing with buttercream. Cover cakes with fondant. Use Cake Dividing Set to divide 12 in. cake into 12ths; divide 12ths in half to make a total of 24 divisions. Mark at top and bottom edge. Roll out 1 package of chocolate rolled fondant; cut 24 strips measuring 6 in. long x 3/4 in. wide and attach at division points with water. Roll 24 logs measuring 6 in. x 1/4 in. wide and attach to cake side between strips.

Attach malted milk balls at bottom border of 8 in. cake with melted candy. Roll two fondant logs (approximately 16 in. long) and twist togeth-

It's perfectly proper to pair a playful groom's cake with a more traditional wedding cake. The groom's cake can coordinate with the wedding cake in design but with a masculine flair. Or, the groom can express his style with a cake of different flavors and unique design.

groom's cakes

er to form a rope. Attach with water as bottom border on 12 in. cake. Attach malted milk balls to sides of cake with melted candy. Add dots of melted candy on logs on cake sides.

AT THE RECEPTION: Position loops and streamers with melted candy on cake top.

"Tasteful Tux" Serves 76*
ADVANCE WORK: One day ahead, using patterns on page 120, cut shirt collar and bow tie from fondant rolled 1/4 in. thick. For bow tie, roll a fondant ball for center knot and position. Let dry.

CAKE PREPARATION: Bake and cool two 15 in. heart cakes, 1 1/2 in. high, to create one 3 in. cake. Prepare and cover cake with chocolate fondant.

Position the following fondant pieces immediately after cutting, using patterns on page 120: Roll white fondant about 1/2 in. thick and cut shirt front. Roll chocolate fondant about 1/2 in. thick and cut lapels. Cut buttons using wide end of tip 2A.

To make boutonniere: Tint a 1 in. ball of white fondant moss green. Using cutters in the Step-Saving Rose Bouquet Flower Cutter Set, cut a calyx and leaf from green fondant and cut 2 rose petals from white fondant. Form rosebud boutonniere following instructions in Flower Cutter Set. Position on cake. Position bow tie; attach collar to bow tie with icing.

*Note: Servings listed are for the entire cake.
(For a complete product listing, see page 127.)

cake ornaments & figurines

Cake Ornaments

Wedding cakes began as basic white creations, which relied on only the icing decorations for their ornamentation. By the end of the 1880's, a new look emerged when nearly every wedding cake displayed an elaborately-crafted ornament. Happily, brides today have so many beautiful Wilton ornaments to choose from. Crafted to be treasured for a lifetime, each Wilton ornament is hand-assembled, making it a distinctive keepsake of the wedding day.

A. Victorian Musical Water Globe
Adorned with a trellis of roses, ribbons and doves. Floating glitter sparkles to complement the couple. Plays "The Wedding March". Height: 6 in. Base: $4^1/2$ in. diameter.
215-950

B. A Day To Remember Musical Ornament
Revolving ornament plays "Waltz of the Flowers". Height: 8 in. Base: $4^1/2$ in. diameter.
215-410

C. Always and Forever Musical Ornament
Plays "The Wedding March".
Height: $7^1/4$ in. Base: $4^1/4$ in. diameter.
215-310

D. Topiaries
Classic floral bouquets in sculpted vases reflect today's trend in wedding ceremonies, receptions and millennium celebrations. Ideal for cake tops and centerpieces.
Height: 8 in.

Stephanotis Cascade	103-477
Crinkle Paper Rose	103-479
Ivory Rose	103-474
Blush Rose	103-471
White Rose	103-475
Gold	103-472
Silver	103-476

E. Always And Forever
Resin couple.
Height: $6^1/2$ in. Base: 7 x 5 in. oval.
118-200

F. Pearl Essence
Resin couple.
Height: $8^1/4$ in. Base: 6 in. diameter.
118-607

G. Forevermore
Height: $10^1/2$ in. Base: $4^3/4$ in. diameter.
Black Tux
110-860
Ethnic Couple/Black Tux
110-861

H. Dedication
Height: 7 in. Base: $4^1/2$ x 6 in. oval.
101-150

I. New Beginning
Height: 10 in. Base: $4^1/2$ x 6 in. oval.
110-858

J. Threshold Of Happiness
Resin couple.
Height: 6 in. Base: 6 in. diameter.
118-608

D. Topiaries

E. Always and Forever

F. Pearl Essence

G. Forevermore

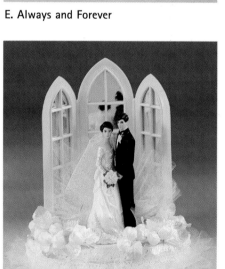

H. Dedication

I. New Beginning

J. Threshold of Happiness

A. Allure

B. Our First Dance

C. Candlelight Romance

D. Romantic Moments

E. Reflections

F. Promise

G. Garden Romance

H. Lustrous Love

I. Splendid

A. **Allure**
Height: 11 in. Base: 5 in. diameter.
101-1783

B. **Our First Dance**
Height: 9^1/$_4$ in. Base: 4^1/$_2$ x 6 in. oval.
118-650

C. **Candlelight Ivory Romance**
Height: 7^1/$_4$ in. Base: 5^3/$_4$ in.
101-415

D. **Romantic Moments**
Height: 10^1/$_2$ in. Base: 4^1/$_2$ x 6 in. oval.
118-651

E. **Reflections**
Porcelain couple. White iridescent.
Height: 8 in. Base: 4^3/$_4$ in. diameter.
117-268

F. **Promise**
Porcelain couple. White.
Height: 9^5/$_8$ in. Base: 4^1/$_2$ in. diameter.
117-315

G. **Garden Romance**
Porcelain couple. White iridescent.
Height: 10^1/$_2$ in. Base: 5 in. diameter.
117-711

H. **Lustrous Love**
Porcelain couple. White.
Height: 8 in. Base: 4^3/$_8$ in. diameter.
117-621

I. **Splendid**
Porcelain couple. White.
Height 10^1/$_2$ in. Base: 4^3/$_4$ in. diameter.
117-506

J. **Simple Joys**
Height: 8 in. Base: 4^1/$_2$ in. diameter.
103-150

K. **Inspiration**
Height: 6^1/$_2$ in. Base: 3^1/$_4$ in. diameter.
106-355

L. **Exuberance**
Height: 7 in. Base: 4^7/$_8$ in. diameter.
103-440

M. **Victorian Charm**
Ivory. Height: 7^1/$_2$ in. Base: 4^1/$_2$ in. diameter.
103-1586

N. **Opulence**
White. Height: 6^1/$_2$ in. Base: 4^1/$_2$ in. diameter.
103-420

O. **Enduring Love**
Height: 5 in. Base: 7 x 5 in. oval.
103-235

J. Simple Joys

K. Inspiration

L. Exuberance

M. Victorian Charm

N. Opulence

O. Enduring Love

A. Mr. & Mrs. Cuddles

B. Country Western

C. Crowning Glory

D. Masterpiece, Ivory

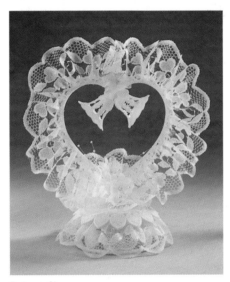

E. Lace Charm

F. Hearts Take Wing

G. Spring Song

H. Circles of Love

I. Sweet Ceremony

A. Mr. & Mrs. Cuddles
Resin couple.
Height: 6$^{1}/_{2}$ in. Base: 4$^{3}/_{4}$ in. diameter.
104-113

B. Country Western
Resin couple. White Tux.
Height: 7 in. Base: 5 in. diameter.
104-112

C. Crowning Glory
White. Height: 9$^{1}/_{2}$ in. Base: 4$^{5}/_{8}$ in. diameter.
103-405

D. Masterpiece
Height: 9$^{1}/_{2}$ in. Base: 4$^{1}/_{2}$ in. diameter.
Ivory 103-425
White 103-430

E. Lace Charm
Height: 11 in. Base: 4$^{3}/_{4}$ in. diameter.
103-151

F. Hearts Take Wing
Height: 10$^{1}/_{2}$ in. Base: 4$^{1}/_{2}$ in. diameter.
103-6218

G. Spring Song
Height: 9$^{1}/_{2}$ in. Base: 4$^{5}/_{8}$ in. diameter.
111-2802

H. Circles Of Love
Height: 10 in. Base: 4$^{5}/_{8}$ in. diameter.
103-9004

I. Sweet Ceremony
Height: 10 in. Base: 4$^{5}/_{8}$ in. diameter.
101-22011

J. Sweetness
Height: 7$^{3}/_{4}$ in. Base: 4$^{1}/_{2}$ in. diameter.
Blonde-haired Bride 101-153
Brown-haired Bride 101-156

K. Expression Of Love
Height: 7$^{3}/_{4}$ in Base: 4$^{1}/_{2}$ in. diameter.
Ethnic Couple 101-933
White Couple 101-931

L. Garden Delight
Height: 10 in. Base: 4$^{3}/_{4}$ in. diameter.
101-1775

M. I Do
Height: 9 in. Base: 4$^{1}/_{2}$ in. diameter.
101-1779

N. Circles Of Love Tier Top
Matches Precious Love ornament.
Height: 3 in. Base: 5 in. diameter.
211-446

Love Birds Tier Top
Matches Love Birds ornament.
Height: 2$^{1}/_{2}$ in. Base: 4 in. diameter.
211-458

Happiness Ribbon Tier Top
Matches Happiness ornament.
Height: 3 in. Base: 5 in. diameter.
211-452

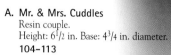

J. Sweetness, Blonde

J. Sweetness, Brown

K. Expression of Love, Ethnic

K. Expression of Love, White

L. Garden Delight

M. I Do

N. Circles of Love Tier Top

Love Birds Tier Top

Happiness Ribbon Tier Top

A.

B.

C.

D.

E.

F.

G.

H.

I.

K.

L.

M.

N.

O.

P.

J.

Petite Wedding Ornaments

Petite in size only, these ornaments are a beautiful addition to cakes used for smaller pre-wedding events. They have the same fine traditional look and quality of our full-sized ornaments. Lovely as table centerpieces and keepsakes for the bridal party.

A. Petite Ribbon Delight
Height: 7$\frac{1}{4}$ in. Base: 3$\frac{1}{4}$ in. diameter.
104-934

B. Petite Heart Of Fancy
Height: 7 in. Base: 3$\frac{1}{4}$ in. diameter.
104-932

C. Petite Lace Trellis
Height: 7$\frac{1}{2}$ in. Base: 3$\frac{1}{4}$ in. diameter.
Ethnic Couple 104-940
White Couple 104-938

D. Petite Double Ring
Height: 7 in. Base 3$\frac{1}{4}$ in. diameter
106-4316

E. Petite Bells Of Joy
Height: 7 in. Base: 3$\frac{1}{4}$ in. diameter.
106-2658

F. Petite Mr. & Mrs. Cuddles
Height: 2$\frac{1}{2}$ in. Base: 3$\frac{1}{4}$ in. diameter.
104-114

G. La Belle Petite
Height: 5$\frac{1}{2}$ in. Base: 3$\frac{1}{4}$ in. diameter.
106-248

H. Petite Spring Song
Height: 7 in. Base 3$\frac{1}{4}$ in. diameter.
106-159

I. Natural Beauty
Height: 6 in. Base: 3$\frac{1}{4}$ in. diameter.
106-1163

J. Petite Romance
Height: 5$\frac{1}{4}$ in. Base: 3$\frac{1}{4}$ in. diameter.
Black Tux   104-942
White Tux   104-941

Fine Figurines

K. With This Ring
Height: 4$\frac{1}{2}$ in. Base: 4 in. diameter.
202-313

L. Threshold Of Happiness
Resin couple. Height: 5 in. Base: 3$\frac{1}{2}$ in. diameter.
202-202

M. Only The Beginning
Resin couple. Light brown skin tone.
Height: 5 in. Base: 3$\frac{1}{2}$ in. diameter.
202-203

N. Together Forever
Porcelain couple. Height: 6$\frac{1}{2}$ in. Base: 4 in. wide by 3 in. deep.
214-415

O. Bianca
Resin couple. Height: 5$\frac{1}{4}$ in. Base: 4 in. diameter.
202-200

P. Always And Forever Petite Embrace
Resin Couple. Height: 3$\frac{3}{4}$ in.
Base: 2$\frac{1}{2}$ in. diameter.
202-311

Q. Stylized Couple
Porcelain couple. Height: $4^5/8$ in. Base: 3 in. wide by $2^1/2$ in. deep.
202-220

R. Inspirational Cross
Crafted in polished resin with finely sculptured scroll and bead highlighting. $4^1/2$ in. high.
202-314

S. First Dance
Height: 6 in.
Black Tux   202-411
White Tux   202-410

T. Love's Duet
Height: 6 in.
Black Tux   202-402
White Tux   202-403

U. Ethnic Love's Duet
Height: 6 in.
202-412

V. Happiest Day
Ethnic couple. Height: $4^1/2$ in.
Black Tux   202-306
White Tux   202-305

W. Our Day
Height: $4^3/4$ in.
Ivory Gown   202-415
White Gown   202-409

X. Petite Happiest Day
Graceful ethnic couple. Height: $3^1/2$ in.
202-404

Y. Lasting Love
Height: $4^1/2$ in.
White Tux   202-303
Black Tux   202-302
Petite Lasting Love (not shown)
Height: $3^1/2$ in.
Black Tux   202-401
White Tux   202-400

Z. Liberated Bride
Height: $4^1/2$ in.
2113-4188
Reluctant Groom
Height: 5 in.
1316-9520

AA. Mr. & Mrs. Cuddles
Resin couple. Height: 4 in.
214-1121
Country & Western
Resin couple. Height: $3^7/8$ in.
214-1120

BB. Mickey and Minnie In Love
Resin couple. Height: $4^1/2$ in.
214-3600
© Disney

Wedding Attendants

CC. Designer Bridesmaids
Many beautiful jewel and soft tones for a myriad of color themes.
Height: $4^1/2$ in. Pk./2

Mint	203-9125
Ruby	203-308
Periwinkle	203-9124
Pearl Blush	203-9123
Pearl Ivory	203-9122
Sapphire (dark blue)	203-9109
Emerald (dark green)	203-9104
Amethyst (purple)	203-9107
Dark Pink	203-9119
White	203-9111
Raspberry (fuchsia)	203-9108
Ethnic Ivory	203-9120
Ethnic White	203-9114

DD. Classic Couple
Height: $4^1/2$ in.
202-8110

EE. Designer Groomsmen
Height: $4^1/2$ in.
White Coat   203-9100   Pk./2
Black Tux   203-9101   Pk./2

FF. Ethnic Designer Groomsmen
Height: $4^1/2$ in.
White Coat   203-9117   Pk./2
Black Tux   203-9116   Pk./2

GG. Ring Bearer
Resin. Height: $3^1/4$ in.
203-7887
Flower Girl
Resin. Height: $3^1/4$ in.
203-7879

Q.

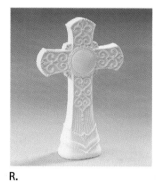

R.

S.

T.

U.

V.

W.

X.

Y.

BB.

Z.

AA.

CC.

DD.

EE.

FF.

GG.

coordinated wedding accessories

It's one of the most important days of your life. Fill it with a collection of wonderful wedding accessories that are matched in their elegant good looks only by their usefulness.

Crystal-Look
The sparkling look of cut crystal was meant for a most glamorous wedding celebration.

A. Fluted Glasses Set
Set with rosebud motif. Height: $8^3/8$ in.
120-708 Set/2

B. Cake Knife & Server Set
Stainless steel with acrylic handles.
120-703 Set/2

C. Crystalique™ Fresh Flower & Unity Candle/Couple Holder
Height: $5^1/4$ in. Base: 2 in. diameter
120-3303

D. Ribbon/Rings Unity Candle
Intricately carved with ring-bearing doves.
9 in. high x $2^3/4$ diameter.
120-710

E. Guest Book
Engraved with silver lettering.
120-800

F. Plume Pen 120-804

G. Heart Bride's Garter
Lace, satin and ribbon trim, with a crystal-look heart.
120-405

H. Toasting Glasses Set
Lilies-of-the-valley design. Height: $4^1/2$ in.
120-203 Set/2

I. Victorian Tri-Unity Candle Holder
Beautiful roses are delicately carved to match Victorian unity candles shown pg. 85.
120-730

J. Ribbon/Rings Unity Candle
120-710

K. Ribbon/Rings Taper Candle Set
Elegant carved detail on clean-burning 10 in. candles.
120-726 Set/2

L.

M.

N.

L. Friendship, Love and Loyalty

The traditional Irish Claddagh design, richly accented in gold, is also rich in tradition—it's been a symbol of Celtic heritage dating back to the 1600's.

Guest Book
Gold-foil embossed cover.
$8^1/2$ in. x $6^1/4$ in.
120–803

Cake Knife and Server Set
Stainless blades, simulated mother-of-pearl handles.
120–706 Set/2

Toasting Glasses Set
Rimmed in gold.
120–206 Set/2

Tri-Unity Candle Holder
Holds unity candle and tapers for the candle lighting ceremony. White finish on heavy-gauge metal.
120–3302

**Friendship, Love and Loyalty
Unity Candle**
Clean-burning with carved gold design.
9 in. high x $2^3/4$ in. diameter.
120–714

Taper Candle Set
10 in. high.
120–724 Set/2

M. Gardenia Keepsake

One of nature's most spectacular and popular flowers, beautifully rendered in handpainted, sculpted resin.

Pen and Holder Set
A charming accessory for signing your guest book.
120–3309

Cake Knife and Server Set
Stainless steel blades with sculpted resin handles.
120–780 Set/2

Frame and Ring Box Set
Frame your wedding invitation or 5 x 7 in. engagement portrait for display at the reception. Ring Box is a dresser accent to hold wedding rings.
120–901

Mini Frames
Favors. $1^3/4$ x 2 in.
1006–215 Pk./12

Gardenia Tri-Unity Candle Holder
Holds unity candle and tapers.
120–3308

Victorian Taper Candles
10 in. ivory candles.
120–722 Set/2

Victorian Unity Candle
Lace motif on this eternal flame. $9^1/2$ in. high x $2^3/4$ in. diameter.
120–712

N. Always and Forever

Truly romantic, this mingling of cherubs, hearts and roses with an iridescent pink hue.

Bride's Garter
Lace with ribbon rosette. Ivory.
120–406

Cake Knife and Server Set
Stainless steel blade.
120–699 Set/2

Fluted Glasses Set
Pearlized pink script and design.
120–709 Set/2

Taper Candle Set
10 in. high.
120–723 Set/2

Unity Candle
$10^1/2$ in. high.
120–713

Unity Candle Holder
2 in. high x $4^3/8$ in. diameter.
120–3304

Plume Pen
120–805

Guest Book
Elegant embossed cover.
120–801

O.

**O. Ring Bearer's
Ribbon Heart Pillow**
Handmade satin pillow trimmed with lace, ribbon and "pearls". 7 in.
120–100

Bride's Garters
Satin band with ribbons, "pearls" and lace. Wide elastic band.
White 120–401
Blue 120–402

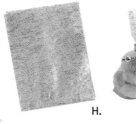

H.

A.

B. Organza Tulle with Ribbon Rose Tie

C. Lurex-Edge Tulle with Ribbon Rose Tie

D. White Tulle with Ribbon Rose Tie

E.

F.

Wedding Crafts

With pretty Wilton accents, it's easy to add personal touches throughout the wedding day. Dress up favors, toasting glasses, centerpieces and more.

A. Pearl Beading
Molded on one continuous 5-yard strand. Remove pearls before cutting and serving cake.

Ivory Small	(4 mm)	211-1983
White Small	(4 mm)	211-1989
White Medium	(6 mm)	211-1990

Tulle Circles
Sheer mesh fabric for elegant puffs and pleated bows. 9 in. diameter.

B. Organza
Scallop-edge; white.
1005-23 Pk./12

C. Gold Lurex-edge   Silver Lurex-edge
1005-21 Pk./12   1005-22 Pk./12

D. White
1005-1   Pk./25

E. Ribbon Rose Ties
For Sachets/Favor Pouches. 6 in. bows on wire ties.
Pk./6

Silver	1006-819	White	1006-822
Gold	1006-818	Ivory	1006-827
Pink	1006-820	Spring Rose	1006-824

Beaded Pearl Ties
5 1/4 in. long. Pk./6

Heart Pearl 1006-828   Pearl 1006-829

F. Champagne Glasses
2 in. high.
Silver 1006-103 Pk./4
Clear 1006-105 Pk./4

G. Pearl Leaf Puff
5 1/2 in. tulle puff with "pearls".
211-1125
Floral Puff Accent
5 1/2 in. tulle puff with soft flowers and "pearl" sprays.
211-1011
Anniversary Bands
3/4 in. diameter.

Silver		Gold	
1006-20	Pk./12	1006-19	Pk./12
1006-101	Pk./48	1006-100	Pk./48

H. Sachets/Favor Pouches
Fill with potpourri, candies, bath oil beads and more. 4 x 3 in.

Solid	1006-171 Pk./4
Translucent	1006-172 Pk./4
Gold Translucent	1006-766 Pk./6
Silver Translucent	1006-767 Pk./6

I. Favor Containers
Round Baskets
2 in. high
1006-113 Pk./4
Flower Carts
4 1/2 in. high
1006-24 Pk./2
Pearl Swans
3 in. high.
1006-108 Pk./4

J. Favor Containers
Scallop Shells
2 in.
1006-28 Pk./4
Filigree Heart Boxes
2 1/4 in.
1006-21 Pk./4
Tuxedo Boxes
4 in. high
1006-48 Pk./2

K. Flower/Rice Basket
Perfect for the flower girl. Lacy design basket holds flower petals or rice for the ceremony; at the reception use it filled with mints or almonds.
Approximately 7 in. high.
1006-603

L. Favor Containers
Small Cowboy Hats
Western accents add a lighthearted touch. 2 1/4 in.
1006-135 Pk./4
Lace Bonnet
4 in. wide.
1006-51
Top Hat and Cane
1 in. high hat; 4 in. cane.
1006-11 Pk./2

M. Place Cards
Use for every life celebration—birthday, religious occasion, shower, wedding, anniversary!
Silver Double Heart
1006-141 Pk./20
Embossed
1006-145 Pk./20

N. Favor Boxes
Great for showers, wedding and anniversary celebrations. Perfect for mints, almonds, potpourri and small gifts.
Silver Heart Pillow
1 in. high x 3 long x 2 1/4 in. wide.
1006-150 Pk./4
Cream Hexagon
2 1/2 in. high x 1 1/4 in. long x 2 1/2 in. wide.
1006-156 Pk./4
White Hexagon
2 1/2 in. high x 1 1/4 in. long x 2 1/2 in. wide.
1006-155 Pk./4
Heart Tab
2 1/4 in. high x 2 1/4 in. long x 2 1/4 in. wide.
1006-157 Pk./4

G.

H. Sachets Filled with Almonds

I.

J.

K.

L.

Ivory Chest
2¹/₂ in. high x 2¹/₄ in. long x 1¹/₂ in. wide.
1006-151 Pk./4

Gold Chest
2¹/₂ in. high x 2¹/₄ in. long x 1¹/₂ in. wide.
1006-152 Pk./4

Silver Chest
2¹/₂ in. high x 2¹/₄ in. long x 1¹/₂ in. wide.
1006-153 Pk./4

O. Silver Metal Favor Baskets
Beautiful and sturdy.
Flower Shape 3³/₄ x 2 in. 1006-160
Heart Mesh 3³/₄ x 2 in. 1006-161
Basketweave 3³/₄ x 2 in. 1006-162
Round 3³/₄ x 2 in. 1006-159

P. Silver Metal Favor Boxes
Ideal keepsake box for jewelry.
Heart 2 x 2 in. 1006-163
Round 2 x 2 in. 1006-164

Q. Favor Bags
Ideal for larger gifts such as mini frames.
5¹/₄ x 3 x 2 in.
Gold 1006-771
Silver 1006-776

R. Crystal-Look Swan Set
Swans fit together beak to beak, the
necks and heads forming a heart. Height
3 in. Base: 2¹/₄ in. diameter.
202-413 Pk./2

Crystal-Look Petite Swan Set
Height 2 in. Base: 1³/₄ in. diameter.
202-414 Pk./2

O. Silver Metal
Favor Baskets

P. Silver Metal
Favor Boxes

N. Favor
Boxes

R. Crystal-Look
Swan Set

M. Place Cards

A.   B.   C.   D.

Mini Wedding Couples

Add a whimsical touch to bridal showers and wedding celebrations. Collectible quality hand-painted resin.

A. Mini Frog
2 in. high
1006-214

B. Mini Bear
2¹/₂ in. high.
1006-212

C. Black Tuxedo
2¹/₂ in. high.
1006-25

D. Gray Tuxedo
2⁷/₈ in. high.
1006-14

E.

F.

Angels

E. Musical Trio
Harmonious wedding accent. Each 3 in. high.
1001-368 Pk./3

Heavenly Harpists
3¹/₂ in. high.
1001-7029 Pk./4

Card Holders
Great place markers, too. (Cards not included.)
1⁵/₈ x 3³/₈ in. high.
1001-9374 Pk./4

F. Petite Cherubs
Angelic figures add a touch of romance. Height: 2 in.
1006-132 Pk./3

Angelinos
Heavenly addition. 2 in. x 3 in.
1001-504 Pk./6

Angel Duet
Fluttering fancies. Each 2 in. high.
1001-457 Pk./2

Frolicking Cherub
Spreading wedding joy. Height: 5 in.
1001-244

Kneeling Cherub Fountain
Accent with tinted piping gel "water". 4 in. high.
1001-9380 Pk./4

Picks

G. Satin Butterflies
Soft and graceful addition to cakes.
Large (double wing)
1006-808 Pk./2

Medium (single wing)
1006-809 Pk./2

H. Crystalique™ Love Birds
6¹/₄ in. high x 3³/₄ in. wide.
1001-3303

Crystalique™ Butterfly
Butterfly 2¹/₂ in. wide. Pick 2³/₄ in. long.
1001-873 Pk./2

G.

H.

Birds

I. Doves
Small 2 x 1¹/₂ in.
1002-1710 Pk./12

Iridescent
2 in. wide.
1002-509 Pk./6

Glittered
Coated with non-edible glitter. 2 x 1¹/₂ in.
1006-166 Pk./12

J. Petite Song Birds
A note of grace and poise. 2¹/₄ in. high.
1316-1210 Pk./4

Kissing Lovebirds
Beak-to-beak romantics. One piece, 5¹/₂ in. high.
1002-206

Love Doves
Devoted duo provides the perfect finish. 4 x 2³/₄ in.
1002-1806 Pk./2

I.

J.

K. Bubble Bands
Fit around neck of Wilton Wedding Bubbles for an instant decoration. 3/4 in. wide.
Double Pearl Bow
1007-8003 Pk./12

L. Organza Bow Bubble Band
1007-8004 Pk./12

M. Wedding Bubbles
Surround the newly married couple with bubbles for luck! Contains 24 .6 oz. bottles with wands.
1007-8000 Pk./24

Floating Candle Sets
Float these pretty candles in crystal bowls to bring the soft glow of candlelight to bridal showers and wedding day festivities. Set/2

N. Dove
$2^1/4$ in. high
120-765

Swan
$2^1/4$ in. high
120-715

Bell Trio
2 in. high
120-764

Rose Bouquet
2 in. high
120-767

O. Floating Heart Candles
Candles are 13/4 in. high and burn for over 3 hours.

Gold	120-760
Silver	120-761
Ivory	120-763
Pink	120-758
White	120-759

Favor Candles

P. Gift Candles
Look just like wrapped packages. Ideal favors for weddings and showers. $2^1/2$ in. high x $2^1/4$ in. wide x $2^1/4$ in. deep.

Gold	120-450
Silver	120-451
Periwinkle	120-452
Pink	120-453

Q. Wedding Cake Candles
Dazzling replicas of actual Wilton wedding cakes are wonderful gifts for bridal attendants and wedding guests. Regular size are $5^1/2$ in. high and burn for over 8 hours. Petite size are $2^3/4$ in. high and burn for over 3 hours.

Spring Basket
Regular	120-741
Petite	120-745

Rose Bouquet
Regular	120-742
Petite	120-746

Sweetheart
Regular	120-743
Petite	120-747

Rosebud
Regular	120-740
Petite	120-748

K.

L.

M.

N.

O.

P.

Q.

A.

B.

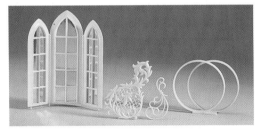

C.

D.

E.

F.

Accents and Bases

A. Filigree Bells*
Beautiful floral detail.
2¼ in. 1001-9439 Pk./6
1⅞ in. 1001-9422 Pk./6
1 in.   1001-9447 Pk./12

Glittered Bells*
A shimmering addition.
1⅞ in. 1007-9088 Pk./6
1 in.   1007-9061 Pk./12

White Frosted Bells*
⅝ in. high. 1006-36 Pk./6

*Ribbon not included.

B. Lacy Hearts
3¾ in. 1004-2306 Pk./12

Filigree Heart Frames
7 x 6½ in. 205-1501 Pk./3
4 x 4 in.   205-1527 Pk./3

Seed Pearl Heart
7 x 6½ in. 205-1006 Pk./3

Crystal-Look Hearts
4¼ in. 205-1672
5½ in. 205-1674

C. 9 in. Lace Fan
Victorian accent makes a wonderful backdrop for your ornament or floral arrangement. Plastic and lace. 9 in. long, opens to 18 in. wide.
1006-601

Gazebo Set
Easy to assemble plastic.
5 x 9 in.
205-8298 Set/6

D. Chapel Windows
Reflective back window setting adds a glimmering effect. Use with base or alone.
6½ x 5 x 1 in. deep.
205-3060

Filigree Swirls
4 x 2¼ in.
1004-2100 Pk./12

Scrolls
2¾ x 11/4 in.
1004-2801 Pk./24

Double Wedding Bands
3½ in. diameter.
201-1008

E. Floral Scroll Base
Richly textured complement to your figurine. Height: 2 in. Base: 4½ in. diameter.
White 201-1303
Ivory 201-305

Romantic Heart Base
2 pieces, 2 base sizes, both 1½ in. high.
Regular 4⅝ in. diameter.
201-7332
Petite 3¼ in. diameter
201-7847

F. Floral Base
Height: 1½ in.
Base: 4⅞ in. diameter.
201-1815

Crystal-Look Base
Height: 1¾ in.
Base: 4½ in. diameter.
201-1450

Oval Base
Bead border. 4½ x 6 in.
201-420

Mirror-Look Oval Base
Create your own ornament with this beautiful reflective base. Sturdy one-piece design holds large figurines, flowers and more. Height: 1¼ in. Base: 5½ in. long x 4 in. wide.
201-529

G. Rose Petals
Fill the flower girl's basket, scatter on the cake table, decorate favors. Lifelike 1¼ in. diameter rose petals add an elegant touch to your wedding day! 1.28 oz. bag.
Blush 1006-774
White 1006-773

Silver Basket
Flower shape sterling silver plated favor basket.
1006-160

G.

Fresh Flower Accessories

H. Floral Figurine Pedestal
Combine fresh or silk flowers and your figurine for a beautiful display. Overall size: 5 in. high x 6 in. wide; pedestal top is 3¼ in. square.
113-3304

I. Crystal-Look Bowl
4½ in. diameter; 1½ in. deep.
205-1404

J. Crystalique™ Fresh Flower and Unity Candle/Couple Holder
Your floral bouquet and unity candle or couple look incredible against the cool texture of this crystal-look base. Height: 5¼ in. Base: 2 in. diameter.
120-3303

K. Flower Spikes
Fill with water, push into cake, add flowers. Makes cakes safe for insertion of stems or wires. 3 in. high.
1008-408 Pk./12

L. Fresh Flower Holders
Insert easily under cake tiers to hold cascading blooms, greenery, pearl sprays, tulle puffs and more. Use with floral oasis to keep flowers looking fresh.
205-8500 Pk./2

M. Crystalique™ Ribbon Arch Fresh Flower Holder
Ribbon loops grace this beautifully frosted design and allow for fresh or silk flowers to cascade. The base is designed to set into the cake layer after marking and trimming. Height: 7½ in. Base: 5½ in. diameter.
113-3303

Flower Sprays

Exquisite floral and decorative accents to personalize the wedding celebration. Add to toasting glasses, centerpieces, ornaments, bridal apparel. Handcrafted trims include satin, fabric flowers, ribbon, faux pearls.

N. Star Flower
4 in. long.
1006-500

Hanging Lily
8 in. long.
1006-501 Pk./3

Apple Blossom
12 in. long.
1006-502

Lily Pearl
9 in. long.
1006-503 Pk./12

White Pearl
8 in. long.
1006-506 Pk./12

Rose Flower
3½ in. wide.
1006-507

O. Dove on Stems
1¼ in. wide.
1006-18 Pk./6

"Pearl" Hearts
4½ in. long.
1006-35 Pk./6

"Pearl"
4 in. long.
1006-31 Pk./4

Stamens
3 in.
1006-30 Pk./12

Artificial Leaves

Look so natural! Green or white fabric, gold or silver foil. Add to ornaments, centerpieces, bridal floral arrangements and favors.

P. Green Single
2½ in. leaf, 2¼ in. stem.
1005-401 Pk./12

Green
1¼ in. wide.
1005-7570 Pk./72

1⅞ in. wide.
1005-7555 Pk./72

Gold
1¼ in. wide.
1005-6712 Pk./144

1⅞ in. wide.
1005-6518 Pk./144

Silver
1¼ in. wide.
1005-6720 Pk./144

1⅞ in. wide.
1005-6526 Pk./144

White
1⅞ in. wide.
1005-7565 Pk./72

White Triple
2 in. leaf, 3 in. stem.
1005-400 Pk./12

Green Triple
2 in. leaf, 3 in. stem.
1005-402 Pk./12

Pearl Leaves
"Pearl"-edged tulle punctuated with a solo flower. 2¼ in. long.
211-1201 Pk./2

H.   I.   J.

K.

L.   M.

N.

O.

P.

A. Garden Cake Stand

Our beautiful Garden Cake Stand echoes the wrought-iron look found in many formal gardens. Simply place cakes on plates and set on the stand. Painted metal stand is 23 in. high x 22 in. wide and uses any standard 10 in., 14 in. and 18 in separator plates. Satellite garden cake stand sold separately.

307-860

Satellite Garden Cake Stand

Carry on the garden motif to additional cakes. Painted metal stand holds a 12 in. separator plate.

307-861

A.

B. Candlelight Cake Stand

Great size for smaller weddings! Simple, graceful design reinforced with a crossbar for more support. Sturdy, enameled metal design holds up to 40 lbs. Ideal for three stacked tiers supported by a 14 in. separator plate Stand is $21^1/2$ in. diameter ($13^1/4$ in. center cake area) x 5 in. high and uses standard $^7/8$ in. candles. Tapers sold separately.

307-871

B.

C. Floating Tiers Cake Stand Set

Your guests will be captivated by the dramatic illusion of decorated tiers suspended in mid-air. Set includes 17 in. high metal stand; 8, 12 and 16 in. smooth separator plates; instructions.

307-825 Set/4

Additional plates available, see Wilton Yearbook.

C.

D. Crystal-Clear Cake Divider Set
Sparkling clear twist legs beautifully complement your cake. Designed for towering cakes from 6 in. to 14 in. diameter. An elegant combination with Wilton crystal-look accessories. Clear plastic twist legs penetrate cake and rest on plate (dowel rods not needed). Includes 6, 8, 10, 12, 14 and 16 in. plastic separator plates plus 24 legs.
301-9450 Set/30

Additional plates available, see Wilton Yearbook.

E. Tall Tier Cake Stand
Majestically displays your cake at its best! The optional Lady Windemere-look base which uses multiple small cakes as the base tier adds a distinctive look to your wedding reception.

Basic Set
For multi-tiered cakes up to 6 tiers high. Pretty lace-look plates enhance cake designs and hold tiers from 6 in. to 16 in. diameter. Easier to assemble than pillar construction, the twist-together center columns and stong, inter changeable plates provide stability. Set includes five twist-apart columns $6^{1}/_{2}$ in. high with one bottom and one top bolt; 18 in. footed base plate; 8, 10, 12, 14 and 16 in. separator plates (interchangeable, except footed base plate). Plastic.
304-7915 Set/13

Additional plates, columns and replacement parts available, see Wilton Yearbook.

F. Lady Windermere-Look 4 Arm Base
Easily adds 4 base cakes to your tall tier cake. The 4-arm base can be used with any plate from the basic set, except the 18 in. footed base plate. Up to 3 graduated tiers can be added to the cen ter columns. Use the 20 in. diameter 4-arm base with 4 stability pegs, $13^{1}/_{2}$ in. column, bottom column bolt, base bolt and four 12 in. plates. Includes base bolt.
304-8245

Additional base bolt available, see Wilton Yearbook.

G. Rose Separator Ring
The romance of the rose adds an elegant flair to your cake tiers. Use with any Wilton 10 in. Separator Plate Set. No pillars necessary. Made of highly polished, detailed resin. Height: 3 in.; Diameter: 9 in.
303-815

H. Always & Forever Separator Ring
Easily adds a distinctive touch to cake tiers. Use with any Wilton 10 in. Separator Plate Set. No pillars necessary. Made of highly polished, detailed resin. Height: 3 in.; Diameter: 9 in.
303-813

I. Lace Cake Separator Ring
Beautifully scrolled design separates tiers, provid ing an appealing, airy look for garden and can dlelight cakes. Height: 3 in.; Diameter: 9 in.
303-816

J. Super-Strong Cake Stand
Made for heavy base tiers, holds up to 185 pounds of cake. Subtle etched design. High impact polystyrene. Height: $2^{3}/_{4}$ in.; Diameter: 18 in.
307-1200

A.

B.

C.

D.

Cake Kits & Fountains

A. Gazebo Cake Kit
Delicate cuts and trelliswork openings complement garden presentations beautifully. Includes 20 arch and trellis pieces made of strong, coated paper, plus assembly instructions. Use only with: two 10 in. Wilton Separator Plates and four 6$^1/2$ in. Wilton Arched Pillars (top layer) and two 18 in. Wilton Separator Plates and six 13 in. Wilton Arched Pillars (bottom layer). Pillars and plates sold separately.

2104-350

B. Cathedral Cake Kit
Includes: 5 easy-to-assemble white church pieces, 4 white plastic cake supports, a church window that can be illuminated from within. Opening in tower is 8$^1/2$ in. high x 2$^1/2$ in. wide.

2104-2940

C. Fanci Fountain
Economical fountain in crystal-clear design enhances any tiered cake. Adjustable, smooth water flow. Use with 14 in. or larger plates. Quiet 125-250 AC motor with 28 in. cord. Set-up instructions included. Height: 12 in. Diameter: 10 in.

306-2000

Replacement parts available, see Wilton Yearbook.

D. Kolor-Flo Fountain
Professional quality fountain looks spectacular with every tiered cake design. Water cascades dramatically from three levels; simply remove top levels for smaller fountain arrangements. Intricate light system with two bulbs for added brilliance. Use with 14 in. or larger plates, 13 in. or taller pillars for tallest cascade. Coordinates with our 17 in. Crystal-Look Plate Set. Plastic fountain bowl is 9$^3/4$ in. diameter. 110-124V, AC motor with 65 in. cord. Pumps water electrically. Directions and replacement part information included.

306-2599

Replacement parts available, see Wilton Yearbook.

Cascade Set for Kolor-Flo Fountain
Shown on gazebo cake above. Dome shapes redirect water over their surface in non-stop streams. Set includes 4 pieces: 2$^1/2$ in., 4$^1/2$ in., 8 in., and 11$^1/2$ in. diameter (Kolor-Flo Fountain sold separately).

306-1172 Set/4

Stairways & Bridges

E. Crystal Bridge and Graceful Stairway Set
Includes two stairways (16$^3/4$ in. long) and one platform (4$^3/4$ x 5 in.).

Plastic 205-2311 Set/3

One Stairway Only 205-2315

F. Filigree Bridge and Stairway Set
Bridge the gap between lavish tiers. Includes two stairways (16$^3/4$ in. long) and one platform (4$^3/4$ x 5 in.). Plastic.

205-2109 Set/3

One Stairway Only 205-1218

G. Flower Holder Ring
Place at base of Kolor-Flo Fountain. 12$^1/2$ in. diameter x 2 in. high. Plastic.

305-435

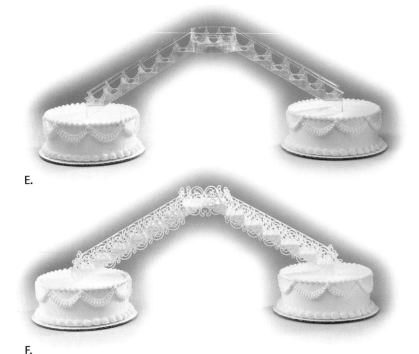

E.

F.

G.

Cake Boards & Trim

Your cake will look its best when presented with quality Wilton boards, doilies and ruffled trims.

I. Ruffle Boards®
Ready-to-use cake board and ruffle in one. Bleached white board and all-white ruffling to complement any cake.

8 in. (for 6 in. round cake)
415-950

10 in. (for 8 in. round cake)
415-960

12 in. (for 10 in. round cake)
415-970

14 in. (for 12 in. round cake)
415-980

16 in. (for 14 in. round cake)
415-990

18 in. (for 16 in. round cake)
415-1000

J. Cake Circles
Corrugated cardboard for strength and stability.

6 in. diameter	2104-64	Pk./10
8 in. diameter	2104-80	Pk./12
10 in. diameter	2104-102	Pk./12
12 in. diameter	2104-129	Pk./8
14 in. diameter	2104-145	Pk./6
16 in. diameter	2104-160	Pk./6

K. Cake Boards
Shaped cakes look best on boards cut to fit. Strong corrugated cardboard in generously sized rectangles. Perfect for sheet and square cakes.

10 x 14 in.	2104-554	Pk./6
13 x 19 in.	2104-552	Pk./6

L. Fanci-Foil Wrap
Serving side has a non-toxic grease-resistant surface. FDA-approved for use with food.
Continuous roll: 20 in. x 15 ft.

Rose	804-124
White	804-191
Gold	804-183
Silver	804-167

M. Doilies
Greaseproof quality for a flawless presentation. Round and rectangular shapes have lace borders sized to fit around your decorated cakes.

Gold Foil

6 in. Round	2104-90306	Pk./18
8 in. Round	2104-90308	Pk./12
10 in. Round	2104-90310	Pk./6
12 in. Round	2104-90312	Pk./4

Silver Foil

6 in. Round	2104-90406	Pk./18
8 in. Round	2104-90408	Pk./12
10 in. Round	2104-90410	Pk./6
12 in. Round	2104-90412	Pk./4

Grease-Proof White

4 in. Round	2104-90204	Pk./30
6 in. Round	2104-90206	Pk./20
8 in. Round	2104-90208	Pk./16
10 in. Round	2104-90210	Pk./10
12 in. Round	2104-90212	Pk./6
14 in. Round	2104-90214	Pk./4
10 x 14 in. Rec.	2104-90224	Pk./6

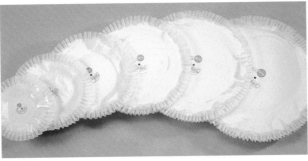

I.

J.

K.

L.

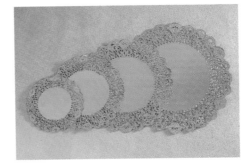

M. Gold

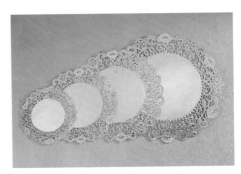

M. Silver

M. White

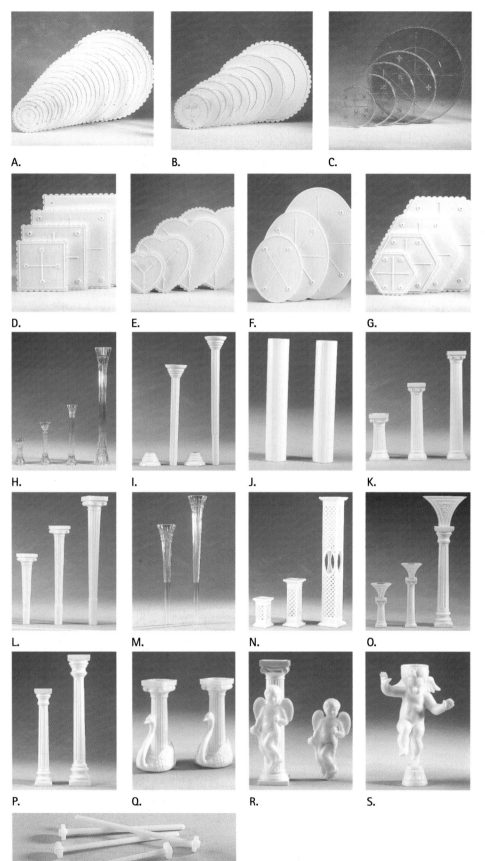

A.

B.

C.

D.

E.

F.

G.

H.

I.

J.

K.

L.

M.

N.

O.

P.

Q.

R.

S.

T.

Separator Plates

A. Decorator Preferred® Separator Plates

Our best, strongest separator plates with the stability and beauty serious cake decorators require. Guaranteed non-breakable. Circles of Strength construction evenly supports all areas of cake.

6 in.	302-6	12 in.	302-12
7 in.	302-7	13 in.	302-13
8 in.	302-8	14 in.	302-14
9 in.	302-9	15 in.	302-15
10 in.	302-10	16 in.	302-16
11 in.	302-11	18 in.	302-18

B. Baker's Best® Disposable Single Plates

Perfect for busy decorators—just use once and toss! Use these sturdy plates with disposable pillars with rings sold below. Recyclable plastic.

6 in.	302-4000	10 in.	302-4004
7 in.	302-4001	12 in.	302-4006
8 in.	302-4002	14 in.	302-4008
9 in.	302-4003		

C. Crystal-look Plates

Use with crystal-look pillars sold below.

7 in.	302-2013	13 in.	302-2078
9 in.	302-2035	*17 in.	302-1810
11 in.	302-2051		

*Use only with 13³/4 in. crystal pillars.

D. Square Separator Plates

7 in.	302-1004	11 in.	302-1047
9 in.	302-1020	13 in.	302-1063

E. Heart Separator Plates

8 in.	302-2112
11 in.	302-2114
14¹/2 in.	302-2116
16¹/2 in.	302-2118

F. Oval Separator Plates

8¹/2 x 6 in.	302-2130
11¹/2 x 8¹/2 in.	302-2131
14¹/2 x 10³/4 in.	302-2132

G. Hexagon Separator Plates

7 in.	302-1705
10 in.	302-1748
13 in.	302-1764
16 in.	302-1799

H. Crystal-look Pillars

Combine with crystal-look plates and Crystal Bridge and Stairway Set (sold on pg. 94).

3 in.	303-2171	Pk./4
5 in.	303-2196	Pk./4
7 in.	303-2197	Pk./4
*13³/4 in.	303-2242	

*Sold singly. Use only with 17 in. crystal plate sold above.

I. Disposable Pillars with Rings

7 in.	303-4000	Pk./4
9 in.	303-4001	Pk./4

J. "Hidden" Pillars

Designed to separate cake tiers slightly and create a floating illusion. Pushed into tiers as dowel rods, they fit onto all white separator plates except Tall Tier. Trimmable, hollow plastic. 6 in. high.

303-8 Pk./4

K. Grecian Pillars

Elegantly scrolled and ribbed.

3 in.	303-3606	Pk./4
5 in.	303-3703	Pk./4
7 in.	303-3705	Pk./4

L. Grecian Spiked Pillars

No need for separator plates on tier tops—push into cake to rest on plate or cake circle beneath. Wide bottom for increased stability.

5 in.	303-3708	Pk./4
7 in.	303-3710	Pk./4
9 in.	303-3712	Pk./4

M. Crystal-Look Spiked Pillars
Push into cake to rest on separator plate or cake circle beneath. Double cake circles for extra support.
7 in. 303-2322 Pk./4
9 in. 303-2324 Pk./4

N. Lattice Columns
Flattering garden-inspired designs.
3 in. 303-2131 Pk./4
5 in. 303-2151 Pk./4
13 in. 303-2113

O. Arched Pillars
Grecian-inspired with arched support.
4^1/$_2$ in. 303-452 Pk./4
6^1/$_2$ in. 303-657 Pk./4
13 in. 303-9720 Pk./2

P. Roman Columns
Handsome pillars may be used with 16 and 18 in. plates and the Kolor-Flo Fountain.
10^1/$_4$ in 303-8136 Pk./2
13^3/$_4$ in. 303-2130 Pk./2

Q. Swan Pillars
Grecian pillars with romantic swan bases add grace to your masterpiece.
Height: 4 in.
303-7725 Pk./4

R. Snap-On Cherub
Accent 5 and 7 in. Grecian Pillars.
Height: 3^1/$_2$ in. 305-4104 Pk./4

S. Dancing Cupid Pillars
A delight for wedding shower or Valentine cakes. Height: 51/2 in.
303-1210 Pk./4

T. Plastic Pegs
Insure that cake layers and separator plates atop cakes stay in place. Pegs do not add support; dowel rod cake properly before using.
Length: 4 in.
399-762 Pk./12

Plate & Pillar Sets

U. Arched Tier Set
Quite dramatic when used with Kolor-Flo Fountain (sold on pg. 94). Includes 14 pieces: Six 13 in. arched columns, two super strong 18 in. round Decorator Preferred separator plates and six angelic cherubs to attach to columns with royal icing or glue. Recommended for use with Gazebo Cake Kit (sold on pg.94).
301-1982

V. Harvest Cherub Separator Set
An idyllic setting for your romantic cake. Pillars snap on to plates for strong support. Set includes 6 pieces: four 7 in. Harvest Cherub pillars and two 9 in. separator plates (lower plate has 12 in. overall diameter).
301-3517

W. Roman Column Tier Set
Includes 8 pieces: six 133/4 in. Roman columns and two strong 18 in. round Decorator Preferred separator plates. Lovely with the Kolor-Flo Fountain (sold on p. 94).
301-1981

X. Crystal-Look Separator Sets
Unique sets add majestic height and sparkling appearance to cakes. Each set includes 6 pieces: two plates and four contoured crystal-look pillars.
7 in. Plate Set; 3 in. Pillars   301-1507
9 in. Plate Set; 5 in. Pillars   301-1509
11 in. Plate Set; 5 in. Pillars   301-1511
13 in. Plate Set; 7 in. Pillars   301-1513
17 in. Plate Set; 13^3/$_4$ in. Pillars 301-1387
Ideal style and height for use with Kolor-Flo Fountain (sold on pg. 94).

U.

V.

W.

X.

Y.

Z.

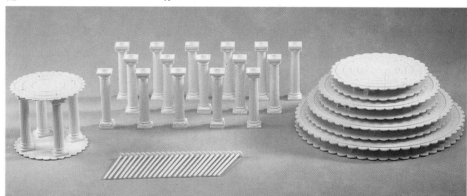

AA.

Y. Classic Separator Sets
Stately Grecian pillars and scalloped-edge plates create beautiful settings for all tiered cakes. Sets include 10 pieces: two Decorator Preferred plates, four pillars and four pegs.
6 in. Plate Set; 3 in. Pillars   2103-639
8 in. Plate Set; 5 in. Pillars   2103-256
10 in. Plate Set; 5 in. Pillars   2103-108
12 in. Plate Set; 5 in. Pillars   2103-124

Z. Plastic Dowel Rods
Heavy-duty hollow plastic provides strong, sanitary support for all tiered cakes. Cut with serrated knife to desired length. Length: 12^3/$_4$ in. Diameter: ^{3}/$_4$ in.
399-801 Pk./4

Wooden Dowel Rods
Cut and sharpen with strong shears and knife. Length: 12 in. Diameter: ^{1}/$_4$ in.
399-1009 Pk./12

AA. Grecian Pillar and Plate Set
A deluxe money-saving collection for the serious cake decorator. Features Decorator Preferred scalloped-edge separator plates and 5 in. pillars. Includes 54 pieces: two each 6 in., 8 in., 10 in., 12 in. and 14 in. plates; 20 Grecian pillars and 24 pegs.
301-8380

Decorator Preferred®

PROFESSIONAL BAKEWARE

The perfect wedding cake must start with the perfect decorating surface. Decorator Preferred is built with more features to help decorators achieve the best results. Straight sides for perfect 90° corners. Superior thickness for the best heat distribution. Pure aluminum construction to bake a light golden brown surface. Batter-fill marks on 3 in. deep square and sheet pans to ensure precise height. You can be sure with Decorator Preferred—the finest materials, the ultimate craftsmanship for the best in baking.

*The May 1999 Good Housekeeping Institute Report rates this Wilton Professional Pan #1 out of 31 different 9 in. round pans.

Rounds

6 x 2 in. deep	2105-6122
8 x 2 in. deep	2105-6136
9 x 2 in. deep	2105-6137
10 x 2 in. deep	2105-6138
12 x 2 in. deep	2105-6139
14 x 2 in. deep	2105-6140
16 x 2 in. deep	2105-6141
6 x 3 in. deep	2105-6106
8 x 3 in. deep	2105-6105
10 x 3 in. deep	2105-6104
12 x 3 in. deep	2105-6103
14 x 3 in. deep	2105-6102
16 x 3 in. deep	2105-6101

Half Round

18 in. x 3 in. deep 2105-6100

3-Pc. Round Sets
6, 10 and 14 in. diameter x 3 in. deep.
2105-6114 Set/3

8, 12 and 16 in. diameter x 3 in. deep.
2105-6115 Set/3

Heating Core
Distributes heat to bake large cakes evenly. Recommended for 3 in. deep pans, 11 in. diameter or larger. Releases easily from cake. $3^1/2$ x $3^1/2$ in. x 4 in. diameter.
417-6100

Squares

8 x 2 in. deep	2105-6142
10 x 2 in. deep	2105-6143
12 x 2 in. deep	2105-6144
14 x 2 in. deep	2105-6145
8 x 3 in. deep	2105-6110
10 x 3 in. deep	2105-6109
12 x 3 in. deep	2105-6108
14 x 3 in. deep	2105-6107

Contours
Create cakes with an elegant, rounded top edge. Perfect shape for positioning rolled fondant.
9 x 3 in. deep 2105-6121

3-Pc. Contour Set
Includes 7, 11, 15 in. pans, 3 in. deep.
2105-6118 Set/3

2-Pc. Contour Set
Includes 9, 13 in. pans, 3 in. deep.
2105-6119 Set/2

Sheets

9 x 13 x 2 in. deep	2105-6146
11 x 15 x 2 in. deep	2105-6147
12 x 18 x 2 in. deep	2105-6148
14 x 22 x 2 in. deep	2105-6149
9 x 13 x 3 in. deep	2105-6113
11 x 15 x 3 in. deep	2105-6112
12 x 18 x 3 in. deep	2105-6111

Bevels
Attractive angled-edge cakes preferred for Lambeth-style decorating. Our unique 5-Pc. Set has the pans bakers need to create a beautiful beveled layer cake, when used with the appropriate-sized round pan.

5-Pc. Bevel Set
Includes 8, 10 and 12 in. top bevel pans, $2^1/2$ in, deep and 14 and 16 in. bottom bevel pans, $1^1/4$ in. deep.
2105-6116 Set/5

10 in. Bevel Top
2105-6117

Tier Pan Sets

Wilton aluminum pan sets will hold their shape, year after year, to help you turn out professional-looking tiers of impeccable form. Our selection of shapes gives you every decorating option. Each pan 2 in. deep, except where noted.

Round Pan Set
Includes 6, 8, 10, 12 in. pans.
2105-2101 Set/4

Round Pan Set, 3 in. Deep
Includes 8, 10, 12, 14 in. pans.
2105-2932 Set/4

Heart Pan Set
The ultimate heart cake is beautiful for showers, weddings and more. Includes 6, $9^{1}/4$, $12^{1}/2$ and $14^{1}/4$ in. pans.
2105-2131 Set/4

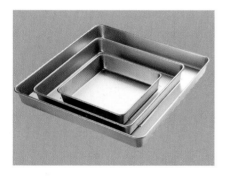

Square Pan Set
Includes 8, 12, 16 in. pans.
2105-2132 Set/3

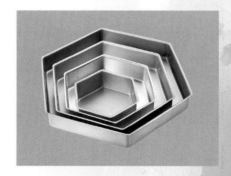

Hexagon Pan Set
Includes 6, 9, 12, 15 in. pans.
2105-3572 Set/4

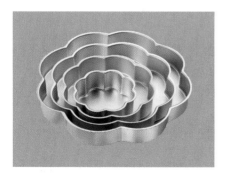

Petal Pan Set
Pretty for showers, weddings and anniversaries.
Includes 6, 9, 12 and 15 in. pans.
2105-2134 Set/4
12 in. only 2105-5117

Oval Pan Set
Includes $7^{3}/4$ x $5^{5}/8$ in.; $10^{3}/4$ x $7^{5}/8$ in.; 13 x $9^{7}/8$ in. and $16^{1}/2$ x $12^{3}/8$ in. pans.
2105-2130 Set/4

Tiered Cake Preparation

A tiered cake is two, three, four or more cakes assembled as one magnificent ensemble. The assembly does require a careful plan. But first, you must carefully bake and prepare the tiers. No amount of skilled decorating can disguise an uneven tier or rough icing. Certain elements of the preparation, such as cake boards between tiers and dowel rods are essential in tiered cake construction.

Baking

Follow recipe directions for recommended batter amounts and specific baking instructions for the pan size you choose.

Prepare the pan by generously greasing the inside with solid vegetable shortening using a pastry brush or paper towel. For best results, do not use butter, margarine or liquid vegetable oil. Spread the shortening so that any indentations are covered. Sprinkle about 2 tablespoons of flour inside the pan and shake so that the flour covers all greased surfaces. Turn the pan upside down and tap lightly to remove excess flour. If any uncovered spots remain, touch up with shortening and flour. Pour batter into pan and place in preheated oven.

After the cake has baked the specific time, remove it from the oven and let it cool in pan on rack for 10 minutes. Run a thin knife between the cake and side of pan. Unmold from pan by placing a cooling rack against the cake and turn both cooling rack and pan over. Lift pan off carefully. Cool at least one hour before icing. Brush off loose crumbs.

Leveling

After the cake has cooled at least one hour, level the top. This can be done in one of two ways.

Using a Serrated Knife
Place the cake on a cake board, then place the board on a Wilton Trim ' n Turn Decorating Turntable.

While slowly rotating the stand, move the knife back and forth across the top of the cake in a sawing motion to remove the crown. Try to keep the knife level as you cut.

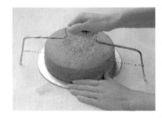

Using the Wilton Cake Leveler
Position the ends of the cutting wire into the notches at the desired height.

With legs standing on the work surface, cut into the crusted edge using an easy sawing motion, then proceed by gently gliding through the cake.

Torting

A serrated knife or the Wilton Cake Leveler also may be used to cut a cake into multiple layers. Torting adds extra height, drama and taste to the cake when the layers are filled with icing, pudding or fruit filling.

Using a Serrated Knife
Measure cake sides and mark with dots of icing or toothpicks all around. Place one hand on top of the cake to hold it steady and rotate the stand.

While slowly turning the cake, move the knife back and forth to cut the cake along the measured marks. Repeat for each additional layer.

Using the Wilton Cake Leveler
Follow the same directions as for leveling.

Separating the Layers
Gently slide a cake circle between layers and lift off. Repeat for each additional layer.

Each tier in the cake, with the exception of the base tier, must be on an uncovered cake circle or board the same size as the tier. This is necessary whether the tier will be positioned on a separator plate, stacked on another tier, or placed on a foil-covered cake board. The board makes it easier to handle the tiers when decorating, offers support for construction and makes it easier to take the cake apart for cutting.

1. Place each cake tier on the same size cake circle. Position the white surface of the board against the cake. Place a few strokes of icing on board to secure the cake in place.

2. If the cake is shaped and you do not have a board to match, cut a board to size using the pan as a pattern.

3. Place the base tier directly on a sturdy base of three or more thicknesses of corrugated cardboard. For increased strength, tape the three layers together, with corrugation lines running in opposite directions. Cover with Fanci-Foil Wrap. For heavy cakes, use 1/4 in. thick fiberboard or plywood.

Filling the Layers

Fill a decorating bag with medium consistency icing and use a large round tip, such as tip 12. Or simply use the coupler without a tip.

1. Starting with the bottom layer, cut side up, create a dam or circle of icing just inside the edge of the cake. Creating a dam is an effective way of preventing the filling from seeping out when the layers are stacked. To create the dam, squeeze a circle about 3/4 in. high and 1/4 in. from the outside edge.

2. Fill the dam with icing, pudding or fruit filling. Place the next layer on top, making sure it is level. The weight of the layer will cause the circle of icing to expand slightly. Repeat until all layers, except the top, are assembled.

3. Position the top layer cut side down, so the top of the cake is perfectly smooth.

The trick to keeping crumbs out of the icing is gliding your spatula on the icing–never allow it to touch the surface of the cake.

Using a Spatula

1. Place a large amount of thin consistency icing on the center of the cake top. Spread across the top, pushing towards edges.

2. Cover the sides with icing. Smooth sides first by holding the spatula upright on a 45° angle with the edge against the cake side, slowly spinning the turntable without lifting the spatula from the cake's side. Return excess icing to the bowl and repeat until sides are smooth.

3. Smooth the top using the edge of the spatula on a 45° angle. Sweep the edge of the spatula from the rim of the cake to its center. Then lift it off and remove excess icing. Rotate the cake slightly and repeat the procedure, starting from a new point on the rim until you have covered the entire top surface. Smooth the center of the cake by leveling the icing with the edge of your spatula. For easier smoothing, it may help to dip the spatula into hot water, wipe dry and glide it across the entire surface. Set the cake aside and allow the icing to crust over for at least 15 minutes before decorating.

Using the Wilton Cake Icer tip

Trim a 16 inch Featherweight bag to fit tip 789. Fill bag half full with icing. Hold bag at 45° angle and lightly press ribbed side of tip against cake.

1. Squeeze a ribbon of icing in a continuous spiral motion to cover cake top, with last ribbon forcing icing over edge of cake top.

2. To ice the sides, squeeze icing as you turn the cake slowly. Repeat the process until the entire cake side is covered.

3. Smooth the sides and top with a spatula, same as above.

Choosing Plastic or Wooden Dowel Rods

Dowel rods are sturdy lengths of rods inserted into the cake to hold up the tiers. Wilton Dowel Rods are available in both plastic and wooden styles. Both types offer food-safe support. The type of dowel rods you choose is simply a matter of preference—experiment with both to choose your favorite!

Plastic Dowel Rods are wider in diameter and offer more support per dowel rod, therefore fewer rods need to be used. They are easy to cut to size with a serrated knife, and many decorators prefer their pure white color. They do take up more cake space, and this should be considered when planning the number of servings.

Wooden Dowel Rods are cut easily and cleanly using sharp shears or a small saw. They are economical and strong.

Adding Dowel Rods to Tiered Cakes

It is absolutely essential to add dowels to tiered cakes to prevent toppled tiers and crushed layers. Use the upper tier for size reference when determining dowel rod placement. All the dowel rods must be placed within the marked area to provide adequate support.

1. Center a cake board the same size as the tier above on base tier and press it gently into icing to imprint an outline. Remove. Use this outline to guide the insertion of the dowel rods*.

2. Insert one dowel rod into cake straight down to the cake board. Make a knife scratch on the rod to mark the exact height. Pull dowel rod out.

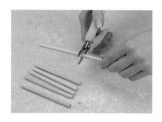

3. Cut the suggested number of rods the exact same length, using the mark on the first one as a guide.

4. Now, insert rods into tier, spacing evenly 1¹/₂ in. in from the imprinted outline. Push straight down until each touches the cake board. Repeat this procedure for every stacked or pillared tier on the cake.

*The general rule for the number of dowel rods to use is–the larger and more numerous the tiers, the more dowels needed. If the tier above is 10 in. or less, use six ¹/₄ in. dowels. Use 8 dowel rods for 16 in. and 18 in. cakes; on these larger cakes, additional rods in the center area may be used for added support. For larger cakes with many tiers, use ¹/₂ in. dowel rods in the base tier. When using white plastic dowel rods that are wider and provide more support, the number needed will be less.

Adding Dowel Rods for Ornaments, Flowers or Decorations

Anytime anything other than regular candles or lightweight toppers are placed on any cake, the area must be reinforced with dowel rods as well to prevent crushed cake tops or the ornament falling off and breaking.

1. Use at least 4 dowel rods evenly spaced around a circle approximately the size of the ornament base.

2. Place a cake board or plate on the tier.

3. Position the ornament.

Nearly every cake design can be adapted to fit any size wedding. Don't let the number of servings determine the look of your cake. If the design of a certain cake does not fit the number of servings needed, simply adjust it to fit the wedding size.

Many brides want the look of a big wedding cake, yet they do not need that many servings for their size reception. Certain cake designs, such as tiers set on pillars, give the illusion of a larger cake. Also, any cake design can be constructed using craft block or cardboard circle dummies. This gives the illusion of a larger cake without increasing serving sizes. If using cardboard circles, stack the amount you need for the desired height, tape together and wrap with foil. Decorate the dummy just like a real cake—first ice and seal with royal icing, then ice and decorate with buttercream icing to match the other tiers. If covering the dummy with fondant, a royal icing sealing is not necessary, but ice lightly in buttercream icing.

Tiered cake designs offer so many decorating possibilities and options for the bride. Using these guidelines and the diagrams on these 2 pages, you will see just how different tier cake combinations can give you the wedding cake of your dreams.

Want more servings?
- Add a larger base tier.
- Increase the size of each tier. For example–change 14, 10 and 6 in. tiers to 16, 12 and 8 in.
- Add satellite cakes. This gives a lavish effect on the reception table. A bonus–the satellite cakes are very easy to serve.
- Have extra cake in the kitchen for extra servings. Sheet cakes are most economical and convenient to serve, and guests will not be able to tell the difference.

Need fewer servings?
- Subtract a tier, usually the base tier.
- Reduce the size of the tiers–change from 16, 12 and 8 in. tiers to 14, 10 and 6 in. tiers.
- Reduce the size of the satellite cakes. Instead of 12 in. satellites, use 10 in. Or reduce a 10 in. satellite to 8 in.

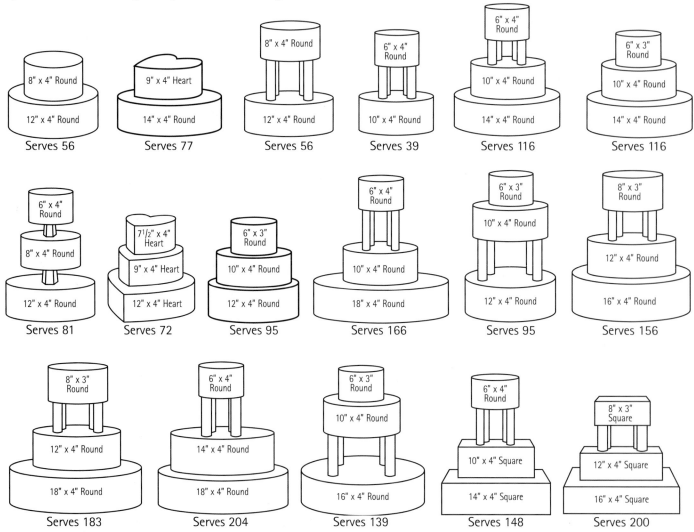

Note that the top tier is often saved for the first anniversary. The number of servings given here does not include the top tier. See page 113, Wedding Cake Data, to determine number of servings for different tier sizes.

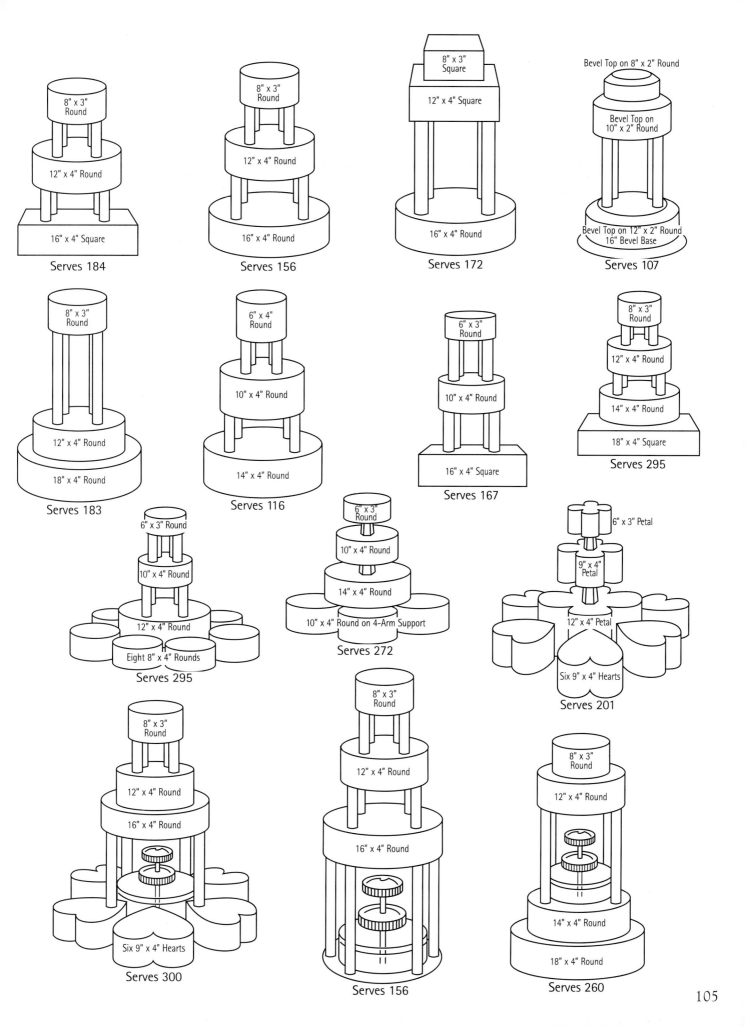

8" x 3" Round
12" x 4" Round
16" x 4" Square
Serves 184

8" x 3" Round
12" x 4" Round
16" x 4" Round
Serves 156

8" x 3" Square
12" x 4" Square
16" x 4" Round
Serves 172

Bevel Top on 8" x 2" Round
Bevel Top on 10" x 2" Round
Bevel Top on 12" x 2" Round
16" Bevel Base
Serves 107

8" x 3" Round
12" x 4" Round
18" x 4" Round
Serves 183

6" x 4" Round
10" x 4" Round
14" x 4" Round
Serves 116

6" x 3" Round
10" x 4" Round
16" x 4" Square
Serves 167

8" x 3" Round
12" x 4" Round
14" x 4" Round
18" x 4" Square
Serves 295

6" x 3" Round
10" x 4" Round
12" x 4" Round
Eight 8" x 4" Rounds
Serves 295

6" x 3" Round
10" x 4" Round
14" x 4" Round
10" x 4" Round on 4-Arm Support
Serves 272

6" x 3" Petal
9" x 4" Petal
12" x 4" Petal
Six 9" x 4" Hearts
Serves 201

8" x 3" Round
12" x 4" Round
16" x 4" Round
Six 9" x 4" Hearts
Serves 300

8" x 3" Round
12" x 4" Round
16" x 4" Round
Serves 156

8" x 3" Round
12" x 4" Round
14" x 4" Round
18" x 4" Round
Serves 260

105

Building Tiered Cakes

Assembling a tiered cake is an exact science. Decorators have developed specific construction setups that take into account size of tiers and methods of support. It is important to understand the different type of cake setups and the physics behind them. Unsteady support combined with the force of gravity has toppled many a wedding cake–make sure it does not happen to you!

A Sense of Proportion
Creating a tiered cake, which is attractive and architecturally sound, depends on proper proportion. A cake can be two, three, four or more tiers. One or more sets of pillars can divide tiers from each other. Or cakes may be simply stacked together, with support from cake circles and dowel rods. Each wedding tier is usually two layers (total 3 or 4 inches deep). Arranging the tiers in ascending diameter or width gives you pleasing proportion and structural strength. A general rule to follow is keeping a 4 inch difference between tier sizes. For example, a 6 inch tier atop a 10 inch tier above a 14 inch tier. However, depending on the style of cake, a 2 inch difference can work well. The plates used to separate tiers should be one size larger than the cake they support and one size smaller than the cake on which it rests. To separate a 6 inch and 10 inch tier, use an 8 inch separator plate. Pillar height is determined by what will be placed between the tiers, or simply by the design of the cake.

Types and Methods of Tier Cake Construction
Tiered cake assembly may be done in 6 ways, and the following pages explore each one. The purpose of each method is to support the weight of the tiers. Careful planning, preparation and assembly will ensure that the cake will rise steadily and safely from bottom to top.

Refer to pg. 100-103 for instructions on how to prepare the tiers for tiered construction.

Stacked Construction

Using dowel rods and cake boards

Most architectural method of tiered cake construction—tiers are placed directly on top of one another and pillars are not used.

1. Dowel rod all tiers except top tier.

2. Position the middle tier on the base tier, centering exactly.

3. Repeat with the top tier.

4. To stabilize tiers further, sharpen one end of a wooden dowel rod and push it through all tiers and cake boards to the base of the bottom tier.

5. To decorate, start at the top and work down.

Using any type of Wilton Push-In Pillars and plates

Simple assembly–no dowel rods needed!

1. Mark tier for push-in pillar placement. Using the separator plate for the next tier above, gently press it onto the tier, feet down, making sure it is centered. Lift plate away. The feet will leave marks on the icing to guide the position of pillars when you assemble the tier. Repeat this process for each tier, working from largest to smallest tier. The top tier is left unmarked.

2. Place each tier on its separator plate, securing with icing.

3. Position push-in pillars at marks, and insert into tiers. Push straight down until pillars touch the cake board.

4. To assemble, start with the tier above the base tier. Place the feet of the separator plate on the pillar openings.

5. Continue adding tiers in the same way until the cake is completely assembled.

Using separator plates and pillars

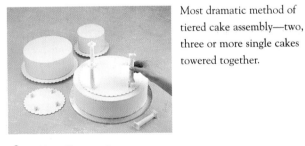

Most dramatic method of tiered cake assembly—two, three or more single cakes towered together.

1. Dowel rod tiers and set tiers on matching size separator plates. (Note: separator plates connected by pillars must always be the same size in diameter).

2. Position separator plates on tiers with feet up.

3. Position pillars over feet on separator plates.

4. Carefully set plated cake on pillars. Continue adding tiers this way.

Wilton Separator Rings

Raise tiers to beautiful heights using Wilton Separator Rings instead of pillars and this cake assembly! Wilton Separator Rings raise the tier 3 inches and are designed to be used with any Wilton 10 in. Separator Plate Set. Prepare the tiers as above, then position the ring instead of the pillars between the separator plates. Separator Rings are available in three beautiful designs to match every wedding cake theme-Rose Garden–full of roses and romance, Always & Forever–highlighted with cherubs and hearts, and Lace Cake–with an airy, garden look.

Combination Pillar and Stacked Construction

Use any combination of dowel rods, boards & separator plates and pillars.

Versatile and beautiful set-up using a combination of pillars, plates and boards. The key to success is inserting dowel rods accurately at every level for support.

1. Mark all tiers for dowel rod placement using a separator plate (for pillar tiers) or a cake circle (for stacked tiers) the same size as the tier above. Insert dowel rods.

2. Position tiers that will be on pillars on matching separator plates (Note: separator plates connected by pillars must always be the same size in diameter).

3. Starting at the bottom level, stack tiers (see p. 106)

4. Position the separator plate (feet up) that will support the tier on pillars.

5. Position pillars over feet.

6. Carefully position the plated tier on the pillars.

Cake Stands

What's the easiest way to create a beautiful, towering tiered cake? With a Wilton Cake Stand, of course! Not only does a cake stand accentuate the beauty, design and size of your wedding cake, but each level of the cake is completely supported, eliminating the need for pillars with separator plates.

Create the dramatic illusion of tiers suspended in mid-air with the **Floating Tiers Cake Stand Set**. Includes 17 in. high metal stand, 8, 12, and 16 in. smooth edge separator plates and instructions.

The **Garden Cake Stand** echoes the wrought-iron look found in many formal gardens–perfect with added flowers and greenery. Painted metal stand is 23 in. high by 22 in. wide. Use with any standard 10 in., 14 in. and 18 in. separator plates. Satellite stands also available.

The **Candlelight Cake Stand** brings the soft glow of candlelight that heightens the beauty of the cake. Romantic swirls of scrollwork with heart design crafted in enameled metal holds up to 40 lbs.—ideal for three stacked tiers supported by your 14 in. separator plate. Stand is $21^{1}/_{2}$ in. diameter ($13^{1}/_{4}$ in. center cake area) x 5 in. high and uses standard $^{7}/_{8}$ in. wide tapers (sold separately).

Easiest way to construct a tier cake.

1. Use boards the same size as tiers, or if tiers are shaped, cut boards to fit. Make a wax paper pattern for each tier except the top tier in order to find the exact center for the columns. Fold the wax paper pattern in quarters. Snip the point to make a center hole. Test the hole for size by slipping it over a column, adjust size if necessary. Trace hole pattern on prepared cake board and cut out.

Also cut a hole in the top tier board to allow for the column cap nut. Save patterns for marking cake tops later.

2. The base tier of the cake will rest on a 16 in. plate. To add legs to this plate, turn it upside down. Using extra strength glue designed for plastic, attach the six legs, positioning the legs over each of the ribs on the plate.

3. Prepare and ice tiers and position on prepared cake boards. Make the center holes in two lower tiers for the columns. Mark the top of the cakes with the corresponding wax paper pattern. Cut the hole by pressing the Cake Corer through the tier right down to the bottom. Hold the corer upright, remove cake corer and push the upper part down to eject the cake center.

4. Attach a 7³/₄ in. column to the prepared base plate with the bottom column bolt from underneath the plate. Slip the 14 in. bottom tier over the column to rest on the plate. Set a 12 in. plate on top of the column.

5. Add a second 7³/₄ in. column and position the 10 in. tier on the plate, slipping it over the column. Finally,

add on 8 in. plate, securing with top column nut. Place the top 6 in. tier on the plate. Mark the backs of all tiers with a dot of icing as a guide when setting up at the reception.

6. To create Lady "Windemere" look. Simply replace the footed base plate and its 7³/₄ in. Column with the Four Arm Base and the 13¹/₂ in. column.

Insert the four spacers into the openings on the underside of the base at the end of the arms. These spacers will keep the base level once the column and the base bolt are added. Glue the spacers in place. Position four identical base cakes on 10 or 12 in. plates, then add desired tiers upward (up to 3 graduated sizes can be added to the center columns).

The brilliance of gently illuminated falling water turns a wedding cake into a spectacular display. The Wilton Kolor-Flo Fountain easily compliments different cake designs in any number of ways—simple planning and careful preparation make this possible!

Assemble the fountain following package directions. It is a good idea to test the fountain before the reception to be certain the water is flowing properly. Be sure the display planned for the fountain will accommodate the height and width of the fountain. Measuring and assembling plates and pillars with the fountain ahead of time will prevent any unpleasant surprises at the reception if the fountain does not fit.

Fountain with Pillars

A versatile arrangement shows the fountain at the bottom of the tiered cake construction. Use with 14 in. or larger plates; 13 in. or taller pillars for tallest cascade. A beautiful display option is to arrange fresh flowers around the base of the fountain, covering the base and the plate. Try setting the base of the fountain inside the Wilton Flower Holder Ring for easier floral arranging (due to space limitations, it's best to use 16 or 18 in. plates when using the Flower Holder Ring).

Fountain on Top of the Cake

This majestic display showcases the fountain as an eye-catching cake top ornament at its best! May be used with stacked or pillar cake designs, be certain that the cake is stable and positioned on a sturdy surface. Dowel rod the cake area where the fountain will be positioned and use with any 14 in. or larger separator plate.

Stairways

Impressive, yet easy to work with, stairways are a beautiful way to pull a multi-tiered masterpiece together. Coordinate them to the cake design by covering with icing flowers, or use them as a graceful platform for bridesmaid and groomsman figurines and wedding ornament.*

To Attach the Stairway

Putting stairs together is easy! It's best to have someone hold the stairway as the position of the cakes is adjusted. The assistant can also help check that stairs stand at the proper height in relation to the cakes. Remember two measurements when assembling stairways:

1. For stairways that will not be joined to a bridge, allow for an 8 in. difference in height from top to bottom of stairway.

2. For stairways that will be joined to a bridge, allow for a 7 in. difference in height from top to bottom of stairway.

Stairways Only

Arrange main cake and any satellite cakes in approximate positions. Have assistant hold stairway above cake and shift the cakes as necessary. Gently insert top of stairway into top side of the main cake until the stairway is flush with the side of the cake. Allow bottom of stairway to rest on satellite cake.

Stairways with Bridges

Just slide the tops of the stairways into the slots on the underside of the bridge. Press gently to lock in place. Set main cake and any satellite cakes in approximate position. Ask the assistant to hold the assembled stairway and bridge above the cakes. Shift the satellites as necessary. Gently press the bridge until its base touches the top tier of the main cake. Allow the bottom of the stairway to rest on the satellite cake.

*Note: Be sure to dowel rod area on cake where bridge and stairway will rest if you will be placing figurines, ornaments or flowers on them.

The beauty and color of fresh flowers adds a special impact to cakes. A spray of petunias, a cascade of orchids or a single gardenia bloom looks lovely against a decorated cake background. Some flowers, such as violets, lavender, certain roses and nasturtiums are actually edible and can be positioned on a cake to impart a delicate flavor. Pretty herbs, such as marjoram and lemon balm that have flowered, can also be used.

No matter what flower is chosen, and how it is displayed, certain precautions must be taken when using fresh flowers on cakes.

Many flowers are toxic or poisonous. Never place any flowers or greenery on or near food without first consulting a florist, botanical society or poison control center to be certain that it is safe. Be sure to specify what part of the plant is being used, as some parts of the plant may be safe to use, and others not. Stamens and styles found in a flower's center may cause an allergic reaction; consider removing them from the flowers before use. In addition, many purchased flowers are sprayed with pesticides. Ask for pesticide-free flowers, or use flowers personally grown.

Never put flowers directly on the cake; use separator plates, floral bowls, plastic wrap, waxed paper or doilies to keep the flowers from touching the cake. Never insert stems directly into the cake; use flower spikes.

Wilton has a variety of products to safely hold flowers for display on cakes, including crystal-look bowls, flower spikes, bases, rings, flower/candle holders and more. See the *Wilton Yearbook of Cake Decorating* or your Wilton dealer for the complete selection.

Using Flowers in a Crystal-look Bowl

Silk flowers arranged in a crystal-look bowl are a beautiful alternative to fresh and the arrangement becomes a lasting reminder of your spectacular cake. Assemble using floral foam designed for dry arrangements, and omit the water, of course!

1. Use water-absorbing foam for fresh flowers. Cut foam, soak in water and secure in bowl using waterproof floral tape.

2. Arrange flowers by pushing stems into foam.

3. Position bowl on cake.

Using Flowers in Flower Spikes

Flower Spikes are used for more than just flowers. Use them as a safe and clean way to add all types of other accents to cakes. Spikes can hold trims on wire stems such as doves, hearts, pearl sprays, curled ribbon, bows, tulle puffs, and even balloons.

1. Insert Flower Spikes in cake. Be creative with your arrangements; spikes can be positioned on cake top or sides.

2. Using a small eyedropper, fill spike $1/4$ full of water. Be careful not to overfill or water will spill on cake when flowers are added.

3. Insert flower stems into spikes.

111

More to Know

Storing the Cake

Take some final precautions and store the finished cake the best way possible. After all, time, effort and creativity have made it very special. The best way to protect the cake during storage is by placing it in a clean, covered cake box. Avoid using foil or plastic wrap to cover a decorated cake–these materials can stick to icing and crush delicate decorations.

Beware of the following factors that can affect the look of decorated cakes.
Sunlight or fluorescent lighting will alter icing colors. Keep the cake stored in a covered box and out of direct sunlight.
Humidity can soften royal icing and gum paste decorations. If the climate has high humidity, prepare the royal icing using only pure cane confectioners' sugar (not dextrose or beet sugar), add less liquid and add 1 teaspoon more Meringue Powder to the recipe).
Heat will melt icing and cause decorations to droop. Keep the decorated cake as cool as possible and stabilize buttercream icing by adding 2 teaspoons Meringue Powder per recipe.

Transporting a Tier Cake

Moving a tier cake from one location to another can be a challenge. Follow these guidelines and the cake will arrive safely–whether you are traveling hundreds of miles or just a few.

Be sure the cake is constructed on a sturdy base. As outlined on page 101, Positioning Tiers on Boards, base tiers must be placed on a base made of three or more corrugated cake boards. Place the base tiers of larger cakes on a fiberboard or plywood base 1/4 in. thick. Cakes on pillars must be transported unassembled. Toppers, candles and ornaments should not be placed on the cake during transport. Take tiers apart if constructed in Center Column or Push-in Leg method. Leave columns or legs in place. Position the plates on crumpled foil or in shallow pans if they do not sit level. Remove pillars from Dowel and Pillar cakes; plates stay in position. For stacked cakes, move the entire assembled cake. For a combination cake, take tiers apart, keeping stacked tiers as units.

Place the cakes in clean, covered, sturdy boxes that are sized to the base of each cake. This will prevent the cake from shifting within the box and possibly crushing the sides of the cake. If the box is too big, remove the cake, roll pieces of masking tape sticky side out and attach to the inside bottom of the box. Position the cake base on top of the tape. The tape will hold the base in place within the box. Place the boxes on carpet foam or a non-skid mat on the floor of the vehicle to prevent shifting. Keep the boxes flat; never place on car seat. Cakes can also be transported in the trunk of the car only if the weather is cool. If the tiers cannot be boxed, they can be transported on large pieces of foam. Make tracings of the bases of all the tiers. Transfer the tracings onto large pieces of soft foam, 3 to 4 inch thick. Use a sharp knife and cut out depressions 1/2 inch deep for each tier. Place the foam on the floor of the vehicle; place the tiers carefully in the depressions in the foam. Drive carefully. At the destination, request a cart on wheels to move the cake into the reception area. This is easier and safer than carrying by hand. Remove the cakes from the boxes on the reception table by cutting the sides of the boxes and sliding the cakes out. Bring along a repair kit–extra icing, prepared decorating bags and tips, flowers –just in case it is necessary to repair any damage at the destination.

Wedding Cake Cutting Guide

This guide shows how to cut popular shaped wedding tiers into pieces approximately 1 in. x 2 in. by two layers high (about 4 in.). Even if a larger serving size is desired, the order of cutting is still the same. The first step in cutting is to remove the top tier, and then begin the cutting with the 2nd tier followed by the 3rd, 4th and so on. The top tier is usually saved for the first anniversary, so it is not calculated into the serving amount.

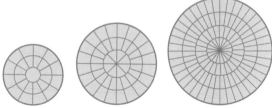

Round Tiers:
Move in two inches from the tier's outer edge; cut a circle and then slice 1 in. pieces within the circle. Now move in another 2 in., cut another circle, slice 1 in. pieces and so on until the tier is completely cut. The center core of each tier and the small top tier can be cut into 1/2ths, 4ths, 6ths, and 8ths, depending on size.

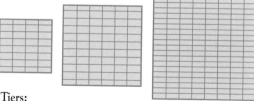

Square Tiers:
Move in 2 in. from the outer edge and cut across. Then slice 1 in. pieces of cake. Now move in another 2 in. and slice again until the entire tier is cut.

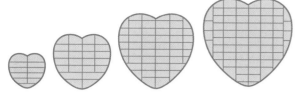

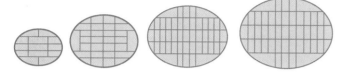

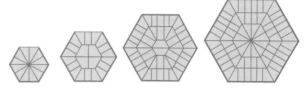

Heart Tiers:
Divide the tiers vertically into $1/2$ths, 4ths, 6ths and 8ths. Within rows, slice 1 in. pieces of cake.

Petal Tiers:
Cut similar to round tiers as diagram shows.

Oval Tiers:
Move in 2 in. from the outer edge and cut across. Then slice 1 in. pieces of cake. Now move in another 2 in. and slice again until the entire tier is cut.

Hexagon Tiers:
Cut similar to round tiers.

Cutting guides for shapes not shown can be found in other Wilton publications.

Wedding Cake Data

Use this chart as a guide when baking wedding cake tiers. Fill pans $1/2$ to $2/3$ full; 3 in. deep pans should be filled only $1/2$ full. Batter amounts on the chart are for pans $2/3$ full of batter. An average 2-layer cake mix yields 4 to 6 cups of batter. For large cakes, always check for doneness after they have baked for one hour. Icing amounts are very general and will vary with consistency, thickness applied and tips used. These amounts allow for top and base borders and a side ruffled border. Number of servings are intended as a guide only.

Decorator Preferred® Bakeware–2 in. Deep Pans

PAN SHAPE	SIZE	# SERVINGS 2 LAYER	CUPS BATTER / 1 LAYER, 2 IN.	BAKING TEMPERATURE	BAKING TIME MINUTES	APPROX. CUPS ICING TO ICE AND DECORATE 2 LAYER CAKE
Oval	$7^3/4$ x $5^3/4$"	13	$2^1/2$	350°	25-30	3
	$10^3/4$ x $7^7/8$"	30	$5^1/2$	350°	25-30	4
	13 x $9^3/4$"	44	8	350°	25-30	$5^1/2$
	16 x $12^3/4$"	70	11	325°	25-30	$7^1/2$
Round	6"	14	2	350°	25-30	3
	8"	25	3	350°	30-35	4
	9"	32	$5^1/3$	350°	30-35	$4^1/2$
	10"	39	6	350°	35-40	5
	12"	56	$7^1/2$	350°	35-40	6
	14"	77	10	325°	50-55	$7^1/4$
	16"	100	15	325°	55-60	$8^3/4$
Round 3" Deep (# Sevings for 1 layer)	8"	15	5	325°	60-65	$4^3/4$
	10"	24	8	325°	75-80	$5^3/4$
	12"	33	11	325°	75-80	7
	14"	45	15	325°	75-80	$7^1/4$
18" Half Round	2" layer	127†	9*	325°	60-65	$10^1/2$
	3" layer	72††	12*	325°	25-65	$10^1/2$
Petal	6"	8	$1^1/2$	350°	25-30	$3^1/2$
	9"	20	$3^1/2$	350°	35-40	6
	12"	38	7	350°	35-40	$7^3/4$
	15"	62	12	325°	50-55	11
Hexagon	6"	12	$1^3/4$	350°	35-40	$2^3/4$
	9"	22	$3^1/2$	350°	35-40	$4^3/4$
	12"	50	6	325°	40-45	$5^3/4$
	15"	72	$11^1/2$	325°	40-45	$8^3/4$
Heart	6"	11	$1^1/2$	350°	25	$2^1/2$
	9"	24	$3^1/2$	350°	30	$4^1/2$
	12"	48	8	350°	30	$5^3/4$
	15"	76	$11^1/2$	325°	40	$8^3/4$
Square	6"	18	2	350°	25-30	$3^1/2$
	8"	32	4	350°	35-40	$4^1/2$
	10"	50	6	350°	35-40	6
	12"	72	10	350°	40-45	$7^1/2$
	14"	98	$13^1/2$	325°	45-50	$9^1/2$
	16"	128	$15^1/2$	325°	45-50	11
	18"	162	18	325°	50-55	13

* Batter for each half round pan † Four half rounds †† Two half rounds

Decorator Preferred® Bakeware–3 in. Deep Pans

PAN SHAPE	SIZE	# SERVINGS 1 LAYER	CUPS BATTER	BAKING TEMPERATURE	BAKING TIME MINUTES
Round	6 x 3"	9	3	350°	35
	8 x 3"	15	5	350°	55-60
	10 x 3"	24	8	325°	65-75
	12 x 3"	33	11	325°	75-85
	14 x 3"	45	15	325°	80-85
	16 x 3"	54	18	325°	75-85
Half Round	18 x 3"	36	12	325°	60-65
Squares	8 x 3"	20	$6^1/2$	350°	55-60
	10 x 3"	27	9	325°	65-75
	12 x 3"	42	14	325°	65-75
	14 x 3"	58	19	350°	65-75
	(Use 2 cores)				
Sheet	9 x 13 x 3"	30	10	325°	60-75
	11 x 15 x 3"	48	16	325°	80-85
	12 x 18 x 3"	60	20	325°	85-90
Contour	7 x 3"	11	$3^1/2$	350°	45-50
	9 x 3"	17	$5^1/2$	350°	45-50
	11 x 3"	24	8	325°	80-85
	13 x 3"	39	13	325°	75-85
	15 x 3"	48	16	325°	75-80
Beveled	8"	9	3	350°	35
	10"	15	5	350°	35
	12"	18	6	350°	45-50
	14"	21	7	325°	45-50
	16"	24	8	325°	45-50

Techniques

Lambeth—Scrolls (from page 55)

To prevent Lambeth decorations from shifting or collapsing from the weight
of the moist icing, pipe one row at a time and allow icing to dry between steps.

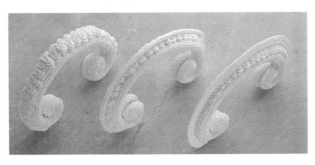

1. Pipe tip 18 zigzag along outside seam of prepared scroll. Let dry.

2. Still using tip 18, pipe line over zigzag. Let dry.

3. Overpipe with tip 5 line, let dry, then add tip 3 line. Let dry completely.

Lattice Pieces (from page 10)

Spray the wax paper covered Flower Former with vegetable oil spray. Lightly wipe with a tissue, leaving a thin film of oil.

Proceed with decorating. When dry, the lattice pieces will remove easily with less chance of breakage.

1. Tape pattern on outside of large flower formers. Cover with waxed paper and tape in place. Spray lightly with vegetable oil spray.

2. Using Royal Icing and tip 3, outline lattice, then pipe diagonal lines in one direction.

Pipe tip 3 diagonal lines running in opposite direction.

3. Pipe bead border around lattice area. Let dry completely.

Bands (from page 55)

Remember to let each line of icing dry before piping another atop it.

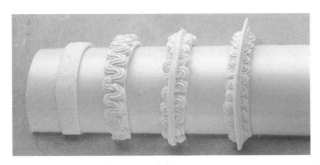

1. Cover the outside of large flower formers with waxed paper. Tape in place. Pipe tip 2B band (smooth side up) over the back of the former. Let dry 48 hours.

2. Cover band with tip 18 zigzag. Let dry, then overpipe with tip 18 line. Let dry.

3. Add tip 5 line, let dry; add tip 3 line. Let dry completely.

The precise, lacy design of this free-hand technique depends on continuous curving strings that do not overlap or touch. The look is more distinctive using a rose tip.

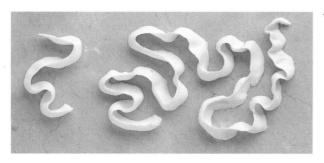

1. Use a stiff to medium consistency icing to insure that decorations will not droop over. Position the tip with wide end down, keep bag level with the decorating surface.

2. Beginning and ending at edges, pipe a continuous string of icing. Vary the direction and curve it around until area is covered. Make certain strings never touch or cross. Don't leave any loose ends. Stop pressure, pull tip away.

Zinnia (from page 67)

For perfectly shaped zinnias, the tip 7 ball should be a bit flatter, more like the shape of a half orange.

1. Use Flower Nail No. 7. Hold decorating bag fitted with tip 7 at 90° angle nail surface. Pipe a ball.

2. Hold decorating bag fitted with tip 101 at 45° angle with the wide end of tip touching the outer edge of the ball. Pipe a row of zigzags for petals. Repeat

for 3-4 more rows, each time angling the tip up a little more.

3. Add five tip 1 dots to center.

Stagecoach (from page 27)

To assure that the glue will stick securely, wipe the prepared stagecoach pieces with a cloth to remove any cornstarch before assembling.

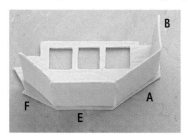

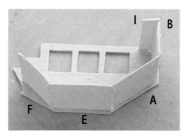

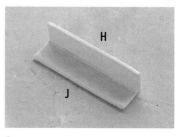

1. Lay one Coach Side Piece flat on table. Use hot glue to attach the following: BOTTOM E side to Coach area E; BOTTOM BACK A side to Coach area A;

BOTTOM FRONT F side to Coach area F; BOTTOM BACK B side to Coach area B.

2. Next, attach piece I side at a right angle to top edge of B.

3. Attach H and J together at a right angle to form bench; let dry separately.

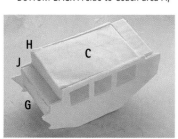

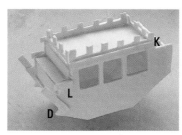

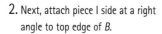

4. Attach G side to Coach area G; attach bench on top of G. Attach the other Coach Side, then attach top C.

5. Add fence pieces around inside of top edges of coach. Attach strips K, L & D to outside of coach.

6. Attach wheels. Using tip 2, pipe bead border and hearts on sides. Brush grated reddish-brown chalk/cornstarch mixture over stagecoach using vertical strokes.

Tassel (from page 69)

Complete and attach one tassel at a time to prevent strips from drying out and cracking.

1. Cut narrow strips 4 in. long x ¼ in. wide, using a small paring knife. For each tassel, use enough strips for a full look. Brush teardrop base with water and attach fondant strips to main tassel area.

2. Roll a ³/₄ in. ball of fondant into an oval; brush with water, and wrap with three ¼ in. wide strips of fondant; trim off excess. Attach with water to top of tassel.

3. Position an additional strip of fondant between the tassel strips and the tassel top to form a wrap; secure with water.

Puffs (from page 69)

Complete one puff at a time to prevent drying.

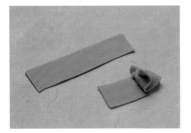

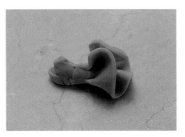

1. Cut fondant into strips—1¹/₂ in x 5 in. for large puffs, 1 in. x 4 in. for small puffs.

2. Gather long end of strip, pinch to secure.

3. Trim excess with scissors. Brush with water to attach to cake. Position small puffs around bottom border, large puffs on cake top.

Side Blossoms (from page 66)

Prepare the fondant for all the blossoms as follows: Combine 1 package of ready-to-use rolled fondant with 1 can of prepared gum paste; tint light yellow. Take a marble size piece of fondant and tint black; divide the remaining yellow mixture into fourths and tint ¼ violet, ¼ peach (add a small amount of rose), ¼ rose (achieve this shade by adding a large amount of rose) and reserve ¼ light yellow.

1. Roll out yellow fondant, using smallest cutters cut 16 blossoms.

2. Position each blossom on foam. Thin petals by rolling ball tool over edges, then cup blossoms by pressing ball tool in center of flower. Set aside to dry. Roll 5 tiny balls of yellow fondant.

3. Attach fondant balls to blossom center with damp brush.

Wipe off cornstarch before assembling blossoms with hot glue.

1. Out of yellow fondant, cut 2 blossoms using smallest cutter and 2 blossoms of the next smallest. Out of peach, rose and violet, cut 1 of each size in each color using the next 3 cutter sizes. Ruffle edges with sharpened dowel rod.

2. Dust pans with cornstarch. Line mini muffin pans with cotton balls and place small blossoms in pan to dry. Dry large blossoms individually on back of the mini muffin pan.

3. Roll small balls of white fondant for centers of small blossoms, roll yellow

for centers of large blossoms. Insert yellow stamens and attach to the smallest blossoms of each color with hot glue. Assemble the blossoms with hot glue, using 3 blossom sizes for each large and 2 for each small.

4. Make 5 stems: bend one end of the florist wire to form 1/4 inch hook.

5. Roll a 3 in. ball of yellow fondant and tint green. Form 5 cone-shaped bases; insert hooked end of wire into each

fondant cone and place into craft block to dry. For large flowers, attach 3 groups of triple leaves with florist tape to flower stems. For small flowers, attach single leaves.

6. Attach stems to flowers using hot glue.

Cheesecake Recipe

Use this recipe for two 6 in. cakes or one 8 in. cake.

Prepare pans: Fit a cake board into the bottom of the springform pan. Wrap outside of the pan with aluminum foil. Butter the sides of the pan (inside only).

Crust:
- 3 1/2 cups graham cracker crumbs
- 3/4 cups sugar
- 1 stick melted butter

Mix ingredients and firmly press mixture into bottom of prepared pan; set aside. Use 1/2 cup to 3/4 cup of crumbs in each 6 in. pan, 1 cup in 8 in. pan. Store remaining crumbs in a plastic bag at room temperature.

Batter:
- 1 3/4 lbs. cream cheese, at room temperature
- 2/3 cups sugar
- 4 eggs
- 14 oz. White Candy Melts®*, coarsely chopped
- 1 tsp. Wilton Clear Vanilla Extract
- 1 1/3 cups whipping cream

Place cream cheese and sugar in mixing bowl. Using electric mixer, cream mixture until smooth. Add eggs, one at a time, while mixing.

Melt White Candy Melts following package directions. Cool 7-10 minutes** Add cooled candy, vanilla and whipping cream to cream cheese mixture. Blend well. Pour batter into prepared pans.

To Bake:

Place each aluminum foil-wrapped pan into a large ovenproof pan or dish. Pour hot water into large pan until it reaches 1/2 in. up sides of pans. Bake in center of a preheated 300° F oven for about 1 3/4 to 2 hours. To test for doneness, gently shake the pan. The top of cake should move as one solid piece. There should be no soupy movement in center. Cake will set completely when refrigerated. Remove from oven to cool. Refrigerate overnight or for 12 hours. To Unmold: Run a straight edge spatula around edge of pan. Release spring and remove ring. Smooth sides of cheesecakes with a wet spatula. Refrigerate until ready to serve. Cakes keep well in refrigerator, well covered, for up to one week.

*brand confectionery coating

**It is important that candy be cooled, but still liquid. If too hot, candy will get lumpy when added to batter.

117

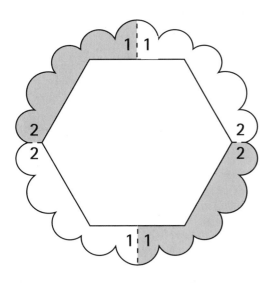

For each tier pattern assembly, place matching numbers at dotted lines as in example for top tier A.

1. Make 4 copies each of patterns A, B and C at actual size.
2. Follow diagram for full pattern assembly, matching numbers at dotted lines. Note: 2 of pattern pieces will have to be flipped, as indicated by the shaded pieces of the diagram.

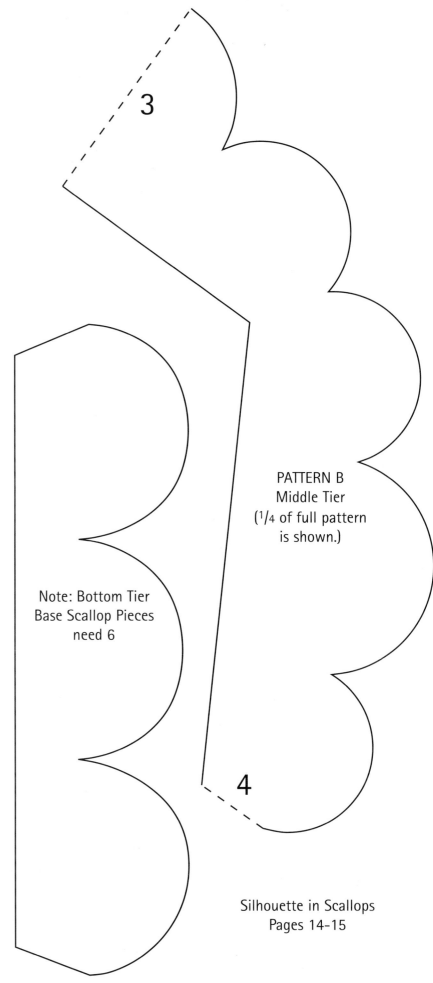

PATTERN B
Middle Tier
($1/4$ of full pattern is shown.)

Note: Bottom Tier Base Scallop Pieces need 6

Silhouette in Scallops
Pages 14-15

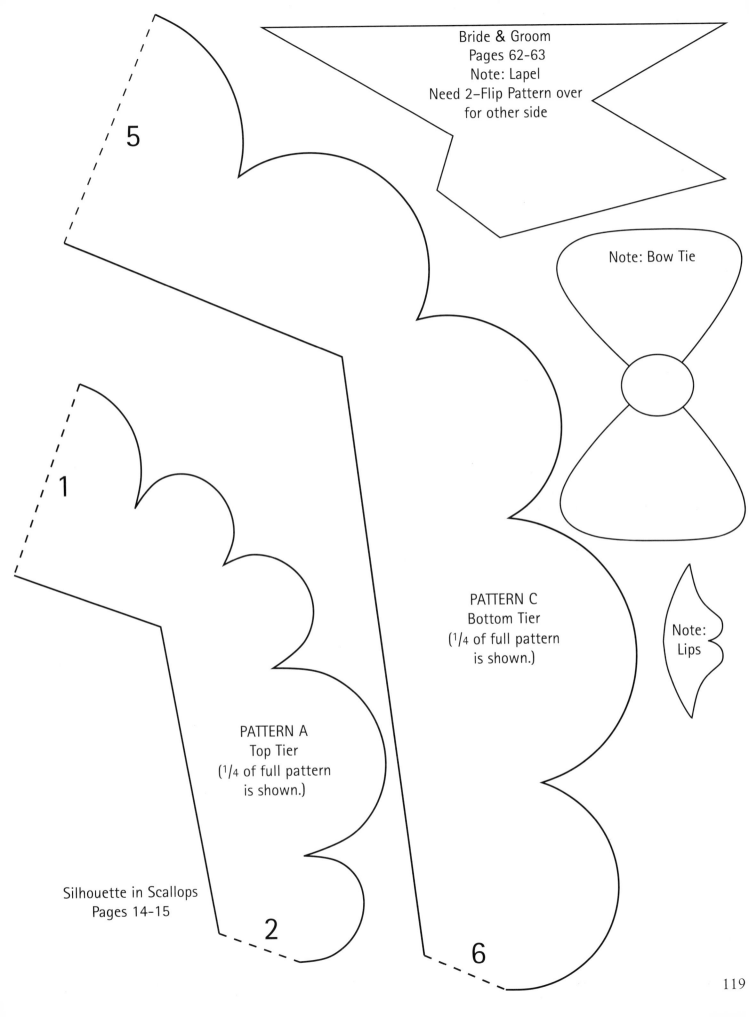

5

1

Bride & Groom
Pages 62-63
Note: Lapel
Need 2-Flip Pattern over
for other side

Note: Bow Tie

PATTERN C
Bottom Tier
(¼ of full pattern
is shown.)

Note:
Lips

PATTERN A
Top Tier
(¼ of full pattern
is shown.)

Silhouette in Scallops
Pages 14-15

2

6

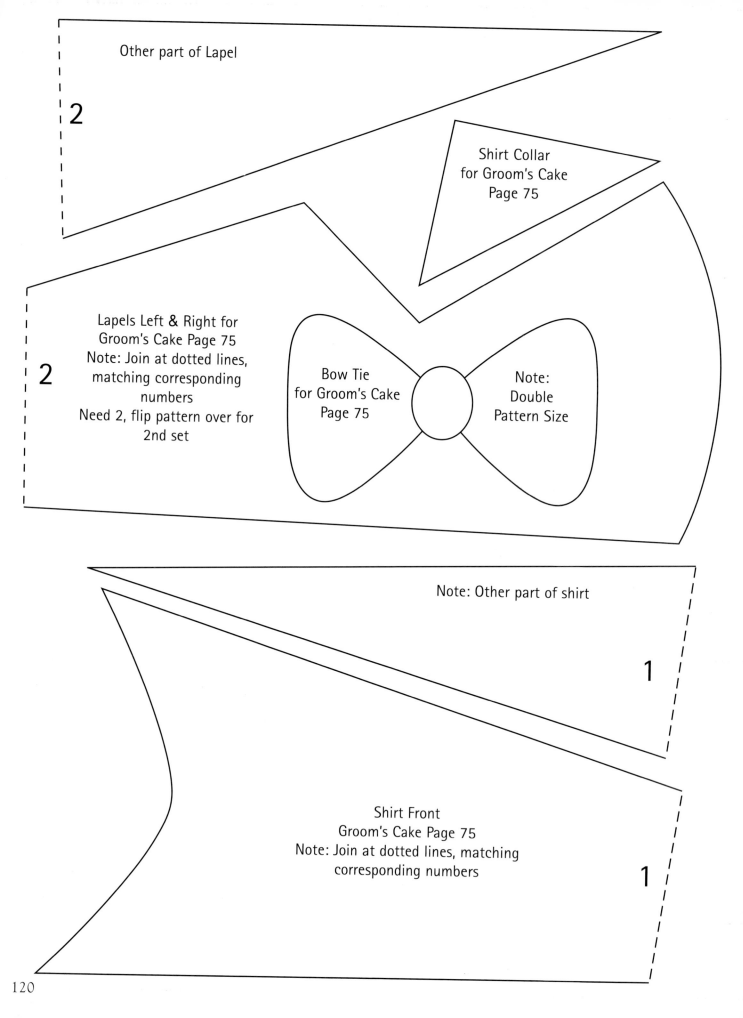

Other part of Lapel

2

Shirt Collar
for Groom's Cake
Page 75

Lapels Left & Right for
Groom's Cake Page 75
Note: Join at dotted lines,
matching corresponding
numbers
Need 2, flip pattern over for
2nd set

2

Bow Tie
for Groom's Cake
Page 75

Note:
Double
Pattern Size

Note: Other part of shirt

1

Shirt Front
Groom's Cake Page 75
Note: Join at dotted lines, matching
corresponding numbers

1

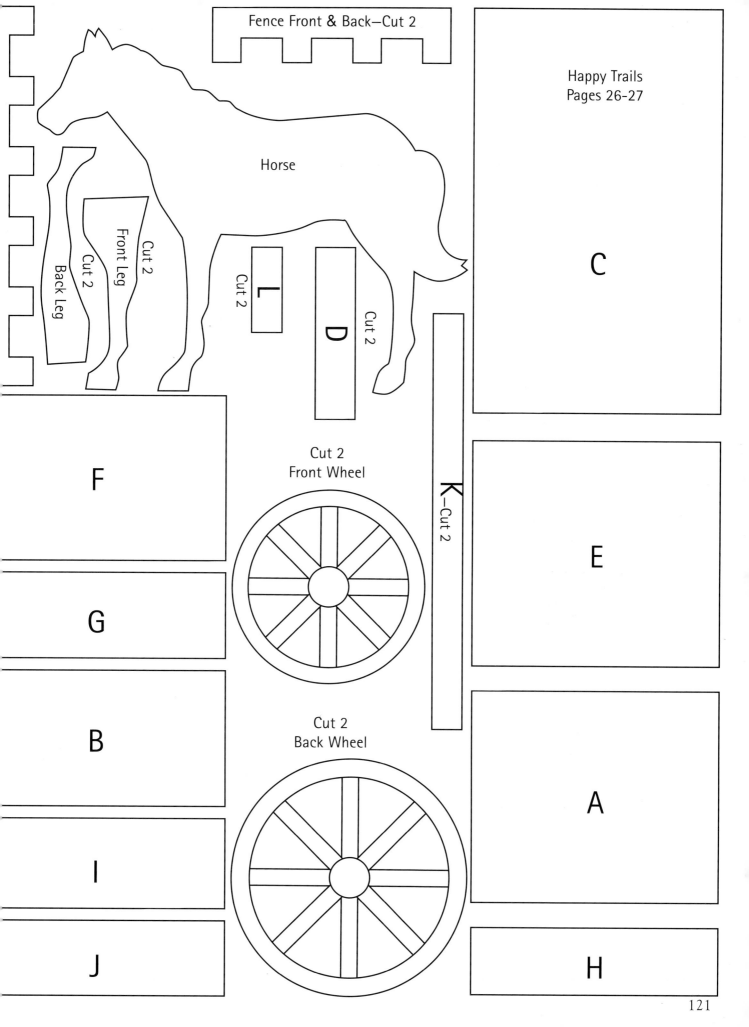

Fence Front & Back—Cut 2

Horse

Front Leg
Cut 2

Back Leg
Cut 2

L
Cut 2

D
Cut 2

Happy Trails
Pages 26-27

C

K –Cut 2

Cut 2
Front Wheel

Cut 2
Back Wheel

F

G

B

I

J

E

A

H

121

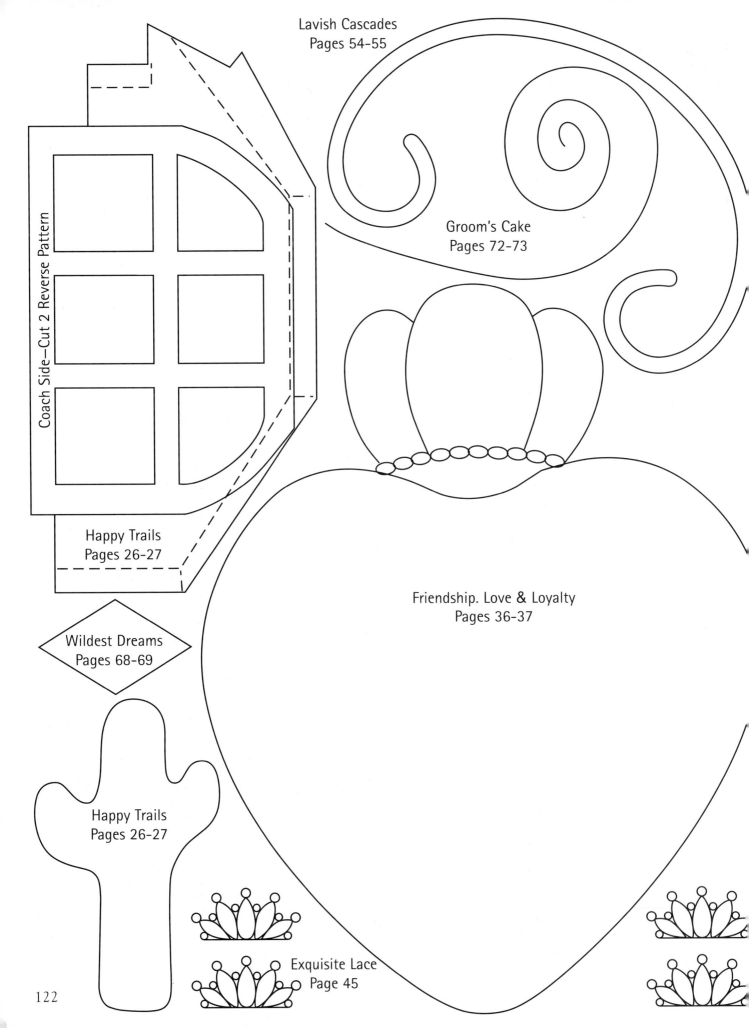

Lavish Cascades
Pages 54-55

Coach Side—Cut 2 Reverse Pattern

Groom's Cake
Pages 72-73

Happy Trails
Pages 26-27

Friendship. Love & Loyalty
Pages 36-37

Wildest Dreams
Pages 68-69

Happy Trails
Pages 26-27

Exquisite Lace
Page 45

Product Checklist

Consult this guide for the decorating products you'll need to complete each project. Wilton has the world's largest selection of quality cake decorating products and wedding cake accessories. Many of these products are sold on pages 76-99 of this book. For a complete selection of Wilton products, see each annual edition of the Wilton Yearbook of Cake Decorating, available at your Wilton dealer.

PHONE IN YOUR CHARGE ORDER TOLL-FREE: 800/794-5866
TOLL-FREE FAX: 888-824-9520
WEBSITE: www.wilton.com
E-MAIL: orders@wilton.com

Love Doves
(p. 7)

6 x 2 in., 10 x 2 in., 14 x 2 in. Round, 18 in. Half Round Pans, p. 98; Spring Song Ornament, p. 80; 9 in. Disposable Pillars, 8 in. Separator Plate, p. 96; Wooden Dowel Rods, p. 97; Small Doves, p. 91; Silver Fanci-Foil Wrap, p. 95; Tip 1B; 20 in. Cake Boards (4 needed); Buttercream Icing; White Florist Wire (22 gauge), Fresh Flowers, 1 1/2 in. Wide White Ribbon (14 yds. needed)

Soft As Gossamer
(p. 9)

3-Pc. Contour Pan Set, p. 98; First Dance Figurine, p. 83; Separator Plates: 8 in. (1 needed), 12 in. (1 needed), 16 in. (2 needed), p. 96; 16 in. Cake Circles, p. 95; 3 in. Grecian Pillars, p. 96; Hidden Pillars (2 pks. needed), p. 96; White Tulle Circles (4 pks. needed), p. 86; White Pearl Sprays (2 pks. needed), Hanging Lily Sprays (11 pks needed), Lily Pearl Sprays (2 pks. needed), p. 91; Golden Yellow Icing Color; Ready-To-Use Rolled Fondant (7 pks. needed); Flower Nail No. 9; Meringue Powder; Decorator Brush Set; Buttercream, Royal Icings, 1 Yard White Tulle, Thin Florist Wire, Waxed Paper Squares

A Dance Of Angels
(p. 10)

6 x 2 in., 10 x 2 in., 14 x 2 in. Round Pans, p. 98; Blush Rose Topiary Ornament, p. 77; Tall Tier Plates: 8 in. (1 needed), 12 in. (5 needed), 16 in. (1 needed); 7 3/4 in. Columns (2 needed); 13 1/2 in. Column (1 needed); 4-Arm Base; Top Column Cap Nut; Bottom Column Bolt, p. 93; Frolicking Cherub (4 needed), p. 88; Petite Cherubs (2 pks. needed), p. 88; Angel Duet (4 pks. needed), p. 88; Plastic Dowel Rods, p. 97; Cake Boards, p. 95; Cake Dividing Set, Garland Marker; Meringue Powder, Tips 2, 3, 5, 18, 101, 102, 103, 352; Cake Corer Tube; Flower Former Set; Flower Nail No. 9; Pink, Creamy Peach, Moss Green Icing Colors; Buttercream, Royal Icings; Waxed Paper, Plastic Ruler, Vegetable Oil Pan Spray, Fresh Flowers

Silver and Gold
(p.12)

6 x 2 in., 10 x 2 in., 14 x 2 in. Round Pans, p. 98; Bianca Figurine, p. 82; Floating Tiers Cake Stand Set, p. 92; 6mm White Pearl Beading (2 pks.), 4 mm White Pearl Beading (4 pks.)*, p. 86; Ready-To-Use Rolled Fondant (6 pks. needed); Easy-Glide Fondant Smoothers; Cake Dividing Set; Tips 2, 4; Royal, Buttercream Icings; Meringue Powder; 3/8 in. Wide Silver Wired Ribbon (9 1/2 yards needed), 1/8 in. Wide Gold Wired Ribbon (12 1/2 yards needed)

*Note: 15 additional pkgs. of 4mm and 6mm pearls were used to decorate table.

Silhouette in Scallops
(p.14)

Hexagon Pan Set (9, 12 and 15 in. needed), p. 99, Splendid Ornament, p. 78, Circles of Love Topper, p. 81; Floral Puff Accents (10 needed), p. 86; 7 in. Grecian Spiked Pillars (3 pks. needed), p. 96; 10 in. and 13 in. Hexagon Separator Plates, p. 96; 1 7/8 in. White Artificial Leaves, p. 91; Cake Board, Fanci-Foil Wrap, p. 95; Color Flow Scallop Patterns, p. 118-119; Tips 1, 2, 4, 13, 104; Flower Nail #9; Buttercream, Royal and Color Flow Icings; Meringue Powder, Color Flow Mix; Mini Marshmallows

Luscious Fruits
(p.17)

8 x 2 in., 12 x 2 in., 16 x 2 in. Round Pans, p. 98; Garden Cake Stand, p. 92; 10, 14, 18 in. Round Decorator Preferred Separator Plates, p. 96; Crystal-Look Bowls (3 needed), p. 91; Tip 104; Wilton Whipped Icing Mix (6 pks. needed); Fresh Strawberries, Blueberries, Raspberries, Mint and Greens; 4 in. Lollipop Sticks, Green Floral Tape

Chocolate Bliss
(p.18-19)

Cake Heart Pan Set (9 1/4 in., 12 1/2 in., 14 1/4 in. needed), p. 99; Our Day Figurine, Ivory Gown, p. 83; Floating Tiers Cake Stand Set, p. 92; Cake Boards, Fanci-Foil Wrap, p. 95; Tips: 2, 21, 127D; Decorating Triangle; Premium Candy Melts® (10 pks. Lt. Cocoa needed), Be Mine Candy Box Kit, Sweetheart Truffles Candy Kit, Hearts Candy Mold; Wilton Ready-To-Use Chocolate Buttercream Icing (or use your favorite recipe)

Centerpieces

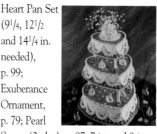

6 x 2 in. Round Pan, p. 98; Singles!® Fancy Ring Mold; Tip 2; Premium Candy Melts®, Lt. Cocoa, (4 pks. needed); Be Mine Candy Box Kit, Deep Heart Truffle Mold, Truffles Candy Mold; Classic Accents Fondant Mold; Disposable Decorating Bags; your favorite candy filling

Serene Swans
(p.20)

Heart Pan Set (9 1/4, 12 1/2 and 14 1/4 in. needed), p. 99; Exuberance Ornament, p. 79; Pearl Swans (2 pks.), p. 87; 7 in. and 9 in. Grecian Spiked Pillars (1 pk. each), p. 96; 11 in. and 14 1/2 in. Heart Separator Plates (2 each), p. 96; Cake Boards, Fanci-Foil Wrap, p. 95; Tips: 2F, 3, 17, 68, 129, Royal Blue, Violet Icing Colors, Buttercream, Royal Icings; Parchment Paper

Product Checklist

Joined in Splendor (p.23)

8 x 2 in., 12 x 2 in., 16 x 2 in. Round Pans, p. 98; Dedication Ornament, p. 77; Dark Pink Designer Bridesmaids (2 pks. needed), Black Tux Designer Groomsmen (2 pks. needed), p. 83; Ring Bearer; Flower Girl, p. 83; 10 in. Round Separator Plates (4 needed), 14 in. Round Separator Plates (2 needed), p. 96; 6¹/₂ in. Arched Pillars (3 pks. needed), p. 97; Filigree Stairways (2 needed), p. 94; Scrolls (4 pks. needed), p. 90; Petite Romantic Heart Base, p. 90; Kolor-Flo Fountain, Flower Holder Ring, p. 94; 1 in. Filigree Bells (3 pks. needed), 2¹/₄ in. Filigree Bells (2 pks. needed), p. 90; Wooden Dowel Rods, p. 97; Cake Boards, Fanci-Foil Wrap, p. 95; Tips 13, 21; Buttercream, Royal Icings; Meringue Powder; Cake Dividing Set; White Tulle, 54 in. Wide x 1 Yard Long; Silk Flowers; Fresh Flowers; 24 Gauge White Florist Wire; Hot Glue Gun

Rich in Roses (p.25)

Oval Pan Set, p. 99; Candlelight Ivory Romance Ornament, p. 78; 8¹/₂ x 6 in. and 11¹/₂ x 8¹/₂ in. Oval Separator Plates, p. 96; 7 in. 9 in. Disposable Pillars (p. 96), Plastic Dowel Rods, p. 97; Cake Boards, Fanci-Foil Wrap, p. 95; Tips 6, 10, 12, 103, 104, 352; Flower Nail #7; Moss Green, Buttercup Yellow Icing Colors; Buttercream, Royal Icings; Meringue Powder

Happy Trails (p.27)

Oval Pan Set (13 x 9 ⁷/₈ in. pan used), p. 99; 14 x 2 in. Square, 14 x 2 in. Round Pan, p. 98; Oval Separator Plates (2 needed), p. 96; 3 in. Grecian Pillars, p. 96; Crystal-Look Bowl, p. 91; Gold Fanci-Foil Wrap, p. 95; Stage Coach, Horse and Cactus Patterns, p. 122; Tips 1, 2, 4; Brown, Moss Green, Ivory Icing Colors; Buttercream, Royal Icings; Meringue Powder; Gum Paste Mix; Ready-To-Use Rolled Fondant (10 pks. needed); 4 in. Lollipop Sticks; Tapered Spatula; Decorator Brush Set, Plywood Board For Base, Non-toxic Chalk, Craft Knife, Scissors, Fresh Flowers, Cornstarch, Hot Glue Gun, Poster Board, Paste, Waxed Paper

Aglow in Candlelight (p.29)

8 x 2 in., 10 x 2 in., 12 x 2 in., 14 x 2 in., 16 x 2 in. Round Pans, p. 98; Lace Charm Ornament, p. 80; Cake Board, Fanci-Foil Wrap, p. 95, Wooden Dowel Rods, p. 97; Tips 3, 17; Buttercream Icing; Cake Dividing Set; Non-drip Pillar Candles; Fresh Flowers

Fountain Fantasy (p.31)

6 x 2 in., 10 x 2 in. Round Pans, Petal Pan Set (15 in. pan used), p. 98/99; Kissing Lovebirds, p. 88; Small White Doves, p. 88; Rose Garden Separator Ring, p. 93; Kolor-Flo Fountain, p. 94; Cake Boards, Fanci-Foil Wrap, p. 95; White Plastic Dowel Rods (3 pks. needed), p. 97 Buttercream, Royal Icings; Ready-To-Use Rolled Fondant (11 pks. needed); Gum Paste Mix; 10 in. Plate from Crystal Clear Cake Divider Set; Confectionery Tool Set; Romance Accents Fondant Mold Set; Step-Saving Rose Bouquet Flower Cutter Set; Flower Former Set; Meringue Powder; Decorator Brush Set; Cornstarch, Round Toothpicks, Triple-thick Cardboard or Plywood Cut For Base Of Cake, Tacky Wax

Cakes For Everyone (p. 33)

Dawn of Romance

7 x 2, 10 x 2, 14 x 2 in. Round Pans, p. 98; Bianca Figurine, p. 82; 6 in. Round Separator Plate, p. 96; Tip 2; Buttercream Icing; Gum Paste Mix; Step-Saving Rose Bouquet Flower Cutter Set; Confectionery Tool Set; Fresh Flowers

Flowing Vines

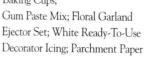

Tall Tier Stand, p. 93; Cake Board, p. 95; Standard Muffin, Mini Muffin Pans; Tips 2, 349, 352; Royal Blue, Violet, Juniper Green Icing Colors; Buttercream Icing; White Standard Baking Cups; Gum Paste Mix; Floral Garland Ejector Set; White Ready-To-Use Decorator Icing; Parchment Paper

Cakes For Everyone (p. 35)

The Loving Couple

11 x 15 in. Sheet Pan, p. 98; Gray Tuxedo Mini Wedding Couple, p. 88; Heart Nesting Cutter Set; Tips: 2, 3, 129, 349; Moss Green Icing Color; Buttercream, Royal Icings; White Candy Melts®; Cooling Grid; Waxed Paper

A Single Rose

Standard, Mini Muffin Pans; Buttercream Icing, Candy Clay

(recipe available in current Wilton Yearbook); Candy Melts®* –Pink, Dark Green, White, Light Cocoa; Cooling Grid; Decorator Brush Set; Real Non-toxic Leaves (rose or lemon), Corn Syrup, Waxed Paper, Vegetable Shortening

Belle Fleurs

11 x 15 in. Sheet Pan, p. 98; Bell Cookie Cutter; Tips 1, 2, 101, 352; Moss Green, Violet Icing Colors; Royal Icing; White Ready-To-Use Decorator Icing; Cooling Grid; ¹/₄ in. Wide x 8 in. Long Satin Ribbon (1 needed for each bow), Waxed Paper

Signature Heart

Mini Heart Pan; Tips 2, 16; Peach, Pink Icing Colors; Buttercream Icing; Ready-To-Use Rolled Fondant; Classic Accents Fondant Mold Set; Cooling Grid; Jelly Roll/Cookie Pan; White Ready-To-Use Decorator Icing; Waxed Paper

Mini Tiers

11 x 15 in. Sheet Pan, p. 98; Comfort Grip™ Tiered Cake Cookie Cutter; Tips 3, 225; Golden Yellow Icing Color; Royal, Buttercream Icings; White Candy Melts®; Bride and Groom Candy Mold; 6 in. Lollipop Sticks; White Ready-To-Use Decorator Icing; Cooling Grid; Waxed Paper, Solid Vegetable Shortening

Doves' Devotion

Doves on Stem, p. 91; Petite Heart Pan; Mini Heart Pan; Tips 4, 101s; Rose Icing Color; Flower Nail No. 9; Poured Fondant, Royal, Buttercream Icings; Waxed Paper

Friendship, Love and Loyalty (p.37)

8 x 3 in., 12 x 3 in. Round Pans, p. 98; Heating Core, p. 98; Threshold of Happiness Figurine, p. 82; Friendship, Love and Loyalty Taper Candle Set (2 sets needed), p. 85; Claddagh Color Flow Pattern, p. 122; 8, 12, 14 in. Separator Plates (one 14 in. and two each 8 and 12 in. needed), p. 96; 5 in., 7 in. Grecian Pillars (1 pk. each), p. 96; Candlelight Cake Stand, p. 92; Tips 2, 3, 13, 17, 224; Buttercream, Royal, Color Flow Icings; Color Flow Mix; Meringue Powder; Decorator Favorites Pattern Press Set (Large and Medium Scroll Pattern used); 8 in. Lollipop Sticks; Decorator Brush Set; Silk Flowers

Rose Canopy (p.39)

6 x 2 in., 8 x 2 in., 10 x 2 in., 14 x 2 in. Round Pans, p. 98; With This Ring Figurine, p. 82; 9 in. Crystal-Look Separator Plates (2 needed), 9 in. Crystal-Look Spiked Pillars (2 sets needed), p. 96; White Plastic Dowel Rods (2 pks. needed), p. 97; Crystal-Look Bowl (2 needed), p. 91; Flower Spikes, p. 91; 2$^1/4$ in. Filigree Bells (1 pk. needed), p. 90; Crystal Bridge and Stairway Set, p. 94; Gold Fanci-Foil Wrap, p. 95; Tips 2, 16, 21; Buttercream Icing; Ready-To-Use

Rolled Fondant (18 pks. needed); Cake Dividing Set; Designer Pattern Press Set; Decorator Brush Set; 8 x 4 in. Craft Blocks (2 needed); Plywood Cut For Cake Base, Florist Foam, Fresh Flowers

Ivory Rose (p.41)

6 x 2 in. 10 x 2 in. Round Pans, p. 98; 5-Pc. Bevel Pan Set (10 in. top bevel, 14 in. bottom bevel base used), p. 98; Ivory Rose Topiary, p. 77; Cake Board, Fanci-Foil Wrap, p. 95; Tips 1, 5, 101s, 349; Buttercream, Royal Icings; Cake Dividing Set; Ready-To-Use Rolled Fondant (7 pks. needed); Planter Fondant Mold Set; Easy-Glide Fondant Smoothers; Quick Ease Fondant Roller

Garden Gala (p.43)

6 x 2 in., 10 x 2 in., 14 x 2 in. Square Pans, p. 98; Love's Duet Figurine, p. 83; Gazebo Set, p. 90; 5 in. Lattice Pillars (2 sets needed), p. 96; 8, 12 in. Square Separator Plates (2 each), p.96; Dowel Rods, p. 97; Tips 1, 2, 3, 5; Leaf Green, Rose, Lemon Yellow, Creamy Peach, Violet, Icing Colors; Royal, Buttercream Icings; Confectionery Tool Set; Gum Paste Floral Collection Flower Making Set; Ready-To-Use Rolled Fondant (9 pks. needed); Meringue Powder; Flower Former Set; Easy-Glide Fondant Smoothers; Paper Towels, Hot Glue Gun

Exquisite Lace (p.44)

7 x 2 in., 10 x 2 in., 14 x 2 in. Round Pans, p. 98;

Forevermore Ornament, p. 77; Lace Pieces Pattern, p. 122; 8, 12, 16 in. Crystal Clear Cake Plates, p. 96; 9 in. Twist Legs (2 pks. needed), p. 96; Hidden Pillars, p. 96; White Pearl Sprays (4 pks. needed), p. 91; Cake Boards, Fanci-Foil Wrap, p. 95; Embossed Heart Pan; Tips 1, 2, 5, 363, 364; Moss Green Icing Color; Buttercream, Royal Icings; Orchid Bouquet Flower Cutter Set; Floral Collection Flower Making Set; Confectionery Tool Set; Ready-To-Use Rolled Fondant (10 pks. needed); Gum Paste Mix (2 cans needed); Flower Former Set; Easy-Glide Fondant Smoothers; Cake Dividing Set; Decorator Brush Set; Meringue Powder; Florist Wire (22-24 gauge), Floral Tape, Non-toxic Pastel Chalk, Cone-shaped Drinking Cup, Cornstarch, Waxed Paper, Vegetable Pan Spray, Craft Block (8 in. square x 2$^1/2$ in. high), Fine Artist Brush

Make it Magical (p.47)

7 x 2 in., 10 x 2 in., 14 x 2 in. Round Pans, 18 in. Half Round Pan, p. 98; Mickey and Minnie In Love Figurine, p. 83; Crystal Clear Cake Divider Set, p. 92; 8 and 12 in. Plates, 7$^1/2$ in., 9 in. Crystal Twist Legs (1 pk. each); Dowel Rods, p. 97; Flower Spikes (2 pks.), p. 91; Cake Boards, Fanci-Foil Wrap, p. 95; Petite Romantic Heart Base (top used), p. 90; Tips 2, 5, 8, 16, 21, 101, 131; Rose, Violet Icing Colors; Buttercream, Royal Icings; Meringue Powder; Flower Nail No. 9; $^3/16$ in. Wide White Curling Ribbon (80 yds. needed); White Florist Wire—32 Gauge x 18 in. Long (480 pieces needed); Floral Tape, Craft Blocks

Fabulous Flavors (p.48)

6 in. and 18 in. Separator Plates (2 each), p. 96; 3 in. Grecian Pillars (2 pks.), 10$^1/4$ in. Roman Columns (2 pks.), p. 96; Cake Boards, Fanci-Foil Wrap, p. 95; Cheesecake Recipe, p. 117; 6 x 3 in., 8 x 3 in. Springform Pans; Muffin Caps® Pan; Tip 366; Buttercream Icing, Disposable Decorating Bags; White Candy Melts® (24 pks.); Small Angled Spatula, Freezer Paper

Ivory Inspiration (p.51)

8 x 2 in., 12 x 2 in., 16 x 2 in. Square Pans, p. 98; Masterpiece Ornament, p. 80; 9, 13 in. Square Separator Plates (2 each needed), p. 96; 5 in. Grecian Pillars (2 pks. needed), p. 96; Plastic Dowel Rods, p. 97; Cake Boards (triple thickness for strength), Fanci-Foil Wrap, p. 95; Tips: 1, 6, 21; Ivory Icing Color; Buttercream Icing; Fresh Flowers

Heart To Heart (p. 52-53)

Honey Bears Heart Pan Set (9$^1/4$, 12$^1/2$ in. pans used), p. 99; Mr. & Mrs. Cuddles Ornament, p. 80; Cake Board, Fanci-Foil Wrap, p. 95; Tips 3, 10, 48, 101s, 104, 127D, 352; Rose, Moss Green Icing Colors; Flower Nail No. 9; Buttercream, Royal Icings; Meringue Powder; Triple Thick Cardboard

Product Checklist

Heart Adoration

Heart Pan Set, (9¼, 12½ and 14¼ in. pans needed) p. 99; Our First Dance Ornament, p. 78; Cake Boards, Fanci-Foil Wrap, p. 95; Tips 1, 2, 5, 12; Rose, Moss Green Icing Colors; Buttercream Icing; Ready-To-Use Rolled Fondant (2 pks. needed); Nesting Heart Perimeter Cookie Cutter Set (largest cutter used); Floral Garland Ejector Set; Decorator Brush Set; 1 in. Thick Board Cut To Fit (approx. 13½ in. diameter); Baby's Breath

Lavish Cascades
(p.55)

18 x 3 in. Half Round, 12 in. x 3 in. Round, 8 in. x 2 in. Pans, p. 98; Only The Beginning Figurine, p. 82; 7 in. Grecian Pillars, 7 in. Separator Plates (2 needed), p. 96; Cake Boards, Fanci-Foil Wrap, p. 95; Dowel Rods, p. 96; Large Scroll Pattern, p. 122; Pearl Stamens (3 pks.), p. 91; Sports Ball Pan; Tips: 2B, 3, 4B, 5, 16, 17, 18, 32, 66, 127, 224; Ivory Icing Color; Buttercream, Royal Icings; Meringue Powder; Lily Nail Set; Flower Former Set; Cake Dividing Set; Aluminum Foil, Pressed Wood Boards for transporting; Waxed Paper, Large White Gum Ball

Butterflies
(p. 56)

Floating On Air
Petal Pan Set (9, 12, and 15 in. pans used), p. 99; Floating Tiers Cake Stand Set, p. 92;

Hidden Pillars, p. 96; Satin Butterflies (2 pks. large; 1 pk. small needed), p. 88; Tips: 4, 13; Creamy Peach, Rose, Golden Yellow Icing Colors; Buttercream Icing; Ready-to-Use Rolled Fondant (2 pks. needed); Quick-Ease Roller; Flower Former Set; Floral Collection Flower Making Set; Confectionery Tool Set; Yellow Colored Sugar; Decorator Brush Set; 1 in. Wide Wire Edge White Ribbon (1½ yds. needed); White Florist Wire; White Florist Tape, Craft Block; Confectioners' Sugar

Butterfly Cupcakes

Large Satin Butterflies (1 pk. needed), p. 88; Tall Tier Cake Stand Set, p. 93; Glue-on Plate Legs (6 needed); 6½ in. Columns (2 needed); 8, 10, 14 in. Separator Plates, p. 96; Standard Muffin Pan; Creamy Peach, Rose Icing Colors; Buttercream Icing; White Standard Baking Cups, Glue

Joyous Rainbow
(p.59)

8 x 2 in., 10 x 2 in., 12 x 2 in., 16 x 2 in. Round Pans, p. 98; Ethnic Love's Duet Ornament, p. 83; Petite Romantic Heart Base, p. 90; Decorator Preferred® Separator Plates—9, 11, 13 in. (2 each needed), p. 96; 5 in. Grecian Pillars (12 needed), p. 96; Dowel Rods, p. 97; Cake Boards, Fanci-Foil Wrap, p. 95; Tip 8; Golden Yellow, Rose, Violet, Kelly Green Icing Colors; Buttercream Icing; Ready-to-Use Rolled Fondant, White (6 pks. needed); Gum Paste Mix (2 cans); Cake Dividing Set, Ruler, Pizza Cutter, Rolling Pin, Cornstarch, Waxed Paper

Blossoms of Love
(p.61)

7 x 2 in., 10 x 2 in., 16 x 2 in. Round Pans, p. 98;

Reflections Ornament, p. 78; Happiness Ribbon Tier Top, p. 81; 11, 17 in. Crystal Plates (2 of each needed), p. 96; 5, 13¾ in. Crystal Pillars (4 of each needed), p. 96; Cascade Set for Kolor-Flo Fountain, p. 94; Kolor-Flo Fountain, p. 94; Flower Ring Holder, p. 94; White Artificial Leaves (2 pks.), p. 91; White Stamens (4 pks.), p. 91; Plastic Dowel Rods, p. 97; Tips 1, 3, 5, 102, 103, 127; Buttercream, Royal Icings; Cake Dividing Set; Lily Nail Set (1¼ and 1⅝ in. nails used); Meringue Powder; Fresh Flowers, Waxed Paper

Bride & Groom
(p.63)

6 x 2 in., 8 x 2 in. Rounds; 10 x 3 in., 12 x 3 in. Rounds, p. 98; Heating Core, p. 98; Mini Wedding Couple Figurine, Black Tuxedo, p. 88; Apple Blossom Flower Spray, p. 91; 5 in. Spiked Pillars, 6 in. Round Separator Plate, p. 96; 6 mm White Pearl

Beading, p. 84; Cake Boards (six 14 in. rounds, three 8 in. rounds), Fanci-Foil Wrap, p. 95; 4 in. Springform; Dowel Rods, p. 97; Patterns: Bride—lips; Groom—bow tie, left and right lapel, tuxedo front, p. 119; Tips 1A, 2, 3, 7, 12, 16, 32, 102, 104, 126, 127D, 352; Buttercream, Royal Icings; Moss Green, Lemon Yellow, Copper (lt. skintone), Black, Pink Icing Colors; Flower Nail No. 7; Ready-To-Use Rolled Fondant, White and Chocolate (5 pks. each); Quick Ease Roller; Decorator Brush Set; Cake Dividing Set; Meringue Powder; ¾ in. Wide White Ribbon (½ yard), White Tulle (1 yard)

Faith & Devotion
(p.65)

Hexagon Pan Set (12, 15 in. pans used), p. 99; Inspirational Cross Figurine, p. 83; Floral Figurine Pedestal, p. 90; Lace Cake Separator Ring, p. 93; Fresh Flower Holders, p. 91; Plastic Dowel Rods, p. 97; Cake Boards, Fanci-Foil Wrap, p. 95; Tulle Circles (3 pks.), p. 86; Tips 2, 5; Buttercream Icing; Floral Oasis, Fresh Flowers

Centerpiece Cakes
(p.66-67)

Vibrant Blooms
Green Triple Artificial Leaves, p. 91; Yellow Stamens (2 pks.), p. 91; Cake Board, Fanci Foil Wrap p. 95;

Wooden Dowel Rods, p. 97; 10 in. Ring Mold, Mini Muffin Pan; Tips 2, 5; Rose, Violet, Golden Yellow, Kelly Green, Black Icing Colors; Buttercream Icing; Lazy Daisy Server; Blossom Nesting Cookie Cutter Set; Gum Paste Mix; Ready-To-Use Rolled Fondant (2 pks.); 11 in. Straight Spatula; 18 mm. Florist Wire, Green Florist Tape, Light Green Tulle, Craft Block, Cornstarch, Corn Syrup, Hot Glue Gun, Toothpicks

Season Of Love
8 x 2 in. Round Pan, p. 98; 6 in., 10 in. Round Separator Plates (2 each needed); 5 in. Grecian Pillars, p. 96; 10¼ in. Roman Columns, p. 96; Cake Board, p. 95; Singles!® 4 x 1¾ in. Non-Stick Springform Pan; Tips 7, 101s; Golden Yellow Icing Color; Buttercream, Royal Icings; Meringue

Powder; Flower Nail No. 9; Fresh
Flowers, Ribbon

Wildest Dreams
(p.69)

6 x 3 in., 8 x 3 in, 12 x 2 in. Round
Pans, 18 in.
Half Round
Pan, p. 98;
Classic Couple
Figurine, p. 83;
Diamond
Pattern, p. 122;
Cake Boards,
Fanci-Foil Wrap, p. 95; one 7 in.,
two 9 in. Decorator Preferred
Separator Plates, p. 96; 9 in.
Disposable Pillars (1 pk.), p. 96;
10 1/4 in. Roman Columns
(1 pk.), p. 96; Hidden Pillars (1 pk.),
p. 96; Plastic Dowel Rods (2 pks.),
p. 97; one standard decorating tip,
any size; Kelly Green, Royal Blue,
Violet, Rose Icing Colors;
Buttercream Icing; Ready-To-Use
Rolled Fondant (14 pks. White);
Cake Dividing Set; Nesting Star
Cookie Cutter Set (2 smallest used);
Decorator Brush Set; Easy-Glide
Fondant Smoothers; 11 3/4 in.
Lollipop Sticks; 22 in. Diameter
Triple-thick Heavy Corrugated
Cardboard or Plywood Base, Scissors,
Plastic Ruler, Small Paring Knife,
Waxed Paper, Cornstarch

Something New, Something Blue
(p. 71)

8 x 3 in.
Round, 12 x 2
in., 14 x 2 in.
Round Pans,
p. 98; Pearl
Essence
Ornament, p. 77; Tall Tier Cake
Plates—14 in. (2 needed), 16 in.
(1 needed), Glue-On Plate Legs
(6 needed), 6 1/2 in. columns (4 need-
ed), Top Column Cap Nut, Bottom
Column Bolt, p. 93; Cake Corer
Tube; 6mm White Pearl Beading
(2 pks.), p. 86; Cake Board, Fanci-
Foil Wrap, p. 95; Wooden Dowel
Rods, p. 97; Tips 1, 1D, 2, 17, 102,

103, 352; Violet, Royal Blue, Moss
Green, Golden Yellow Icing Colors,
Buttercream, Royal Icings; Lily Nail
Set (1 1/4 in. and 1 5/8 in. used),
Meringue Powder; Decorating
Comb; Cake Dividing Set; Waxed
Paper, Aluminum Foil

Groom's Cakes
(p. 72-73)

Sweet Swirls

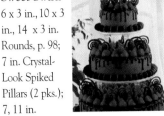

6 x 3 in., 10 x 3
in., 14 x 3 in.
Rounds, p. 98;
7 in. Crystal-
Look Spiked
Pillars (2 pks.);
7, 11 in.
Crystal-Look Separator Plates, p. 96;
Swirl Pieces Pattern, p. 122; Cake
Boards, Fanci-Foil Wrap, p. 95; Tips:
4, 32; Chocolate Buttercream Icing;
Light Cocoa Candy Melts®*
(2 pks.); Chocolate Fudge Canned
Icing (2 cans needed), Fresh
Strawberries

Dessert Chocolates

Light Cocoa Premium Candy
Melts®, (4 bags);
Cordial Cups
Mold,
Parchment
Triangles; Cocoa
Powder, Fresh
Strawberries

Groom's Cakes
(p. 74-75)

Bold Vision

8 x 2 in., 12 x 2
in. Round Pans,
p. 98; Cake
Board, Fanci-
Foil Wrap,
p. 95; Brown
Icing Color;
Chocolate Ready-To-Use Rolled
Fondant (6 pks.); Chocolate
Buttercream; Cake Dividing Set;
Gum Paste Mix (2 cans); Wooden
Dowel Rods; Tapered Spatula, Light
Cocoa Candy Melts® (2 pks.);
Disposable Decorating Bags, Malted
Milk Balls

Tasteful Tuxedo

Heart Pan Set
(14 1/4 in. pan
needed), p. 99;
Cake Boards,
Fanci-Foil
Wrap, p. 95;
Patterns: Lapels,
Bow Tie, Shirt
Front, Collar, p. 120; Moss Green
Icing Color; Tip 2A; Ready-To-Use
Rolled Fondant, Chocolate (3 pks.),
White (1 pk.); Step-Saving Rose
Bouquet Flower Cutter Set; White
Tube Decorating Icing; Chocolate
Buttercream

*brand confectionery coating

There's always something new at Wilton! Fun decorating courses that will help your decorating skills soar. Exciting cake designs to challenge you. Great new decorating products to try. Helpful hints to make your decorating more efficient and successful. Here's how you can keep up to date with what's happening at Wilton.

Decorating Classes

Do you want to learn more about cake decorating, with the personal guidance of a Wilton instructor? Wilton has two ways to help you.

During more than half a century, thousands of students from around the world have learned to decorate cakes with The Wilton Method. In 1929, Dewey McKinley Wilton taught the first small classes in the kitchen of his Chicago home. Today, The Wilton School teaches more people to decorate than any school in the world. As the school has grown, some techniques have been refined and there are more classes to choose from—but the main philosophies of the Wilton Method have remained.

The Wilton School now occupies a new state-of-the-art facility in Darien, Illinois. More than 20 courses are offered each year, including The Master Course, a 2-week class that provides individualized instruction in everything from borders and flowers to constructing a tiered wedding cake. Other courses focus on specific decorating subjects, such as Lambeth and Cakes for Catering. Courses in Gum Paste and Chocolate Artistry feature personal instruction from well-known experts in the field.

For more information or to enroll, write to:

School Secretary, Wilton School of Cake Decorating and Confectionery Art
2240 West 75th Street, Woodridge, IL 60517
Or call: 630-810-2211
For free brochure and schedule

Wilton Class Programs are the convenient way to learn to decorate, close to your home. Our Wilton Method Classes are easy and fun for everyone. You can learn the fundamentals of cake decorating with a Wilton-trained teacher in just four 2-hour classes. When the course is over, you'll know how to decorate star and shell birthday cakes or floral anniversary cakes like a pro. Everyone has a good time—it's a great place for new decorators to discover their talent. Since 1974, hundreds of thousands have enjoyed these courses. Special Project Classes are also available in subjects like candy-making, gingerbread, fondant, cookie blossoms and more.

Call 800-942-8881 for class locations and schedules.

Wilton Products

Visit a Wilton Dealer near you. Your local Wilton Dealer is the best place to see the great variety of cake decorating products made by Wilton. If you are new to decorating, it's a good idea to see these products in person; if you are an experienced decorator, you'll want to visit your Wilton Dealer regularly to have the supplies you need on hand. From bakeware and icing supplies to candles and publications, most Wilton retailers carry a good stock of items needed for decorating. Remember, the selection of products changes with each season, so if you want to decorate cakes in time for upcoming holidays, visit often to stock up on current pans, colors and toppers.

You may also call 800-794-5866 (7WILTON) to place an order. Or, you can place orders at our website, *www.wilton.com*, and by mail, using the Order Form in the Wilton Yearbook of Cake Decorating.

Wilton On The Web

www.wilton.com is the place to find Wilton decorating information on-line. Looking for a fun new cake to make? Our website is filled with great decorating ideas, updated regularly to fit the season. Need a recipe? *www.wilton.com* has delicious desserts and icings to try. Want to save decorating time? There are always helpful hints and answers to common decorating questions. You can also discover new Wilton products and shop for your favorites at *www.wilton.com*.

Wilton Publications

We never run out of decorating ideas! Each year, Wilton publishes several new idea books based on Wilton Method techniques. When you're planning a special occasion, Wilton books are a fantastic source of decorating inspiration.

The Wilton Yearbook of Cake Decorating is our annual showcase of the latest ideas in decorating. Each edition is packed with all-new cake ideas, instructions and products—it's the best place to find out what's new at Wilton. Cakes for every occasion throughout the year are here: holidays, graduations, birthdays, weddings and more. If you're looking for a new cake to test your decorating skills, you can't beat the Yearbook.

Wilton also regularly publishes special interest decorating books, including books on wedding and holiday decorating, candy-making, home entertaining and food gifting. Look for them wherever Wilton products are sold.